Whenever I Fall

Vikki Hammond

ISBN -10 - 1508430322
ISBN-13 – 978-1508430322

Dedication

For Scott, the other half of me, through the good and the bad times we have made it and came out stronger. I love you. You complete me.

And for Beckie, for teaching me it is OK not to be strong all of the time. For loving my children like your own. For catching me when I fell, and for just being you.

Acknowledgements

Kirsty Moseley, without you there would be no book. Thank you from the bottom of my heart.

Katie Stead, for proof reading my book and becoming a friend.

Hilda Reyes, for designing the cover exactly how I wanted it, thank you.

Author's Note

Some names have been changed to protect identities.

THE BEGINNING

We were never supposed to move to Chiltern View, but the house we had been in line for fell through. I think it was fate, though, because just across the road from mine was where my future husband lived.

I had heard a lot about Scott, apparently he had been in trouble with the police and, in a small town, rumours flew around. I was thirteen and quite head strong, he was seventeen and the local bad boy. One day my friends knocked and asked if I wanted to go out for a ride on a motorbike with them down though the fields, feeling bored, I went.

As I walked down the hill, I saw him sat on his bike: curly dark hair hanging in his face, and blueish-green eyes twinkling. He smiled and so did I. We hung around that day all of us laughing and joking and I went home thinking he wasn't so bad after all. Every day was the same in those six weeks' school holidays, I'd hurry to get ready and rush out to meet everyone in the field. The second time I met Scott he asked if I had ever been on a motorbike. When I replied no, he told me to jump on. Though terrified, I obliged, climbing on behind him, holding him tightly leaning in. He reassured me, telling me he would go slowly and that it wasn't a powerful bike so there was nothing to worry about. As we glided through the fields, I felt free. I was instantly hooked on the feeling and felt incredibly safe with Scott. As each day passed I felt myself looking forward to seeing him more and more, butterflies grew in my tummy, although I would never reveal this as I stood no chance; after all, he was older and cool, yet I was still at school!

We got to know each other really well over those next few weeks and one day it happened - he kissed me. We were waiting for our other two friends to come back from their turn on the bike and had been waiting ages. I started messing around flicking bits of wood and stones at him so he got up and we started to play fight. When he tackled me to the floor, I fell and landed straight on top of him. Instantly, he leant forward and kissed me. I kissed him back for two seconds then jumped up, embarrassed and shocked. He told me he had liked me for ages. Confused, I told him I needed to think as everything was moving too fast! I made him wait three days, but finally told him that I would love to be his girlfriend. To this day, he has never let me forget making him wait…

Due to our age, I thought we would probably last a week, but he told me he loved me that very same day and said he always had from the moment he saw me. It was quite intense and unreal how quickly we fell for each other. We spent every spare moment we had together. He used to tell me to set my alarm clock and come over at eight in the morning, and I wouldn't leave his until nine at night. I kept it from my parents for about three months as I was worried about the age gap and his reputation. When they found out, they were extremely worried, but as soon as they met him they could see what I did and grew to love him too.

I wish I could turn back to that carefree summerwhere it was just me and Scott and that bike through the fields, no worries and no stress. Everything was good. I lived with my mum, Pauline, my step dad, Tom, and my two brothers, Thomas and Jamie. Scott lived with his mum and dad a mere stone's throw away. But everything started to change when Scott's parents decided to move to the coast, which left Scott with a choice stay and look for a flat or move with them two hours away. I never expected him to stay; after all, we had only been together a few short weeks. But he said there was no choice, he was staying. He stayed with us - separate rooms, of course, - until he found a flat of his own.

Around this time my granddad passed away. He had started to go downhill when my nan died and was showing signs of, what we thought was, dementia. That was also when the whispering started. If I entered a room in my house my mum and dad would go silent,there was tears and I knew more was going on. I was proved right when I found a book hidden in a drawer, it had the words 'Huntington's disease' on it in bold writing. I wondered why it was hidden and decided to ask my mum. She sat me down.

"This is what your granddad had and died of. It's hereditary, which means I could have it, and so can you and your brothers. You lose the ability to walk, talk and even swallow."

Being young and carefree, I didn't really take in what was being said to me. "It's fine Mum you won't have that," I said. She explained that she was going for the testing but would have to have counselling and tests first.

The day came and off she went to Addenbrookes hospital with my dad, whilst Scott and I watched the boys. I hugged her. "You'll be fine!" I said and waved her off.

She came back through the door just as I was pulling the dinner tray out of the oven;she stood next to my dad straight faced. "I've done dinner so you didn't have to. Boys have been good, Scott's been playing football with them. How did it go?"

She looked at me and I saw her red eyes. "I have it, Vikki, I have the disease."

I gave her a hug said what I thought she wanted to hear, "That's OK. It doesn't mean you will get it though, does it? Not everyone does, they can die of something else unrelated and go through life with no symptoms!" This was to be my first taste of denial but there would be many more situations to come.

Aged fifteen, Scott and I went to visit his parents by the Norfolk coast. As we walked along the beach, he dropped to one knee. "Will you be my wife one day?" I looked at the sea crashing in and this man in front of me on his knees in the sand and thought life doesn't get much better than moments like this. "Yes! Yes, I will marry you!"

My mum had four siblings - two brothers and two sisters - it turned out it was just my mum and one of her sisters that had been diagnosed with Huntingdon's. From that day on, something inside my mum died. I think it was hope. She was never the same after that.

Over the years she stopped laughing for a while, lost her confidence and withdrew into herself, she relied on my dad for a lot. She slept all day and was awake all night, avoiding reality I guess. She still kept her part time job as I think it was her escape. Around this time I was in my second year of college studying childcare when I decided it was time to move out. Scott had his own one bedroom flat he rented privately. Although small, we couldn't even fit an oven in the kitchen or a double bed in the bedroom! It would mean we would be with each other 24/7. I was working at a local supermarket weekends and two nights a week, studying and taking my driving lessons, so had a lot going on. Scott was also working full time but we made time for each other. Working so much, I barely had time for a social life, but when I was invited to an Ann Summers party, I decided to go as I needed some time off to relax. I'm not used to drinking, even to this day… yep I'm a light weight, so why I thought it would be a good idea to have wine shots and alcopops I will never know! I came home – well, was carried home by my friends and was a nightmare the whole night. I drove Scott nuts watching TV with my back to it, repeating how much I loved him and finally falling asleep.

I woke up to the sound of screaming, angry screaming, this guy sounded truly pissed. I was just beginning to get annoyed that the guy had woken me from my deep sleep, but then realised the screaming was coming from Scott. "You puked on me! You puked in my face in your sleep...twice!!!"

I couldn't even open my eyes to look at him but felt lumps in my hair. "Urghhmph," Was my response. Next thing I know I'm being lifted out of bed and feel myself being stripped naked and bunged in the shower, how he held me up and managed to stay calm I will never know. I managed to open my eyes and saw him covered in vomit; it was in his face, hair and all down his chest. After he washed me he put me back to bed and I fell back into a deep sleep.

When I woke again, I instantly ran to the toilet where I virtually stayed for the next twenty-four hours. I had never felt so ill in my life. Everything hurt, my head was pounding and I couldn't keep a single thing down. I called in sick to the college for the next three days whilst I recovered, and thought no more of that day until the following month.

I was sat in the computer room at college when I had this sudden realisation - I was late for my period. I turned to my friend Kristy, "I need to do a pregnancy test. I'm about a week late, I'm never late!" After college we jumped on a bus and headed to the town and I grabbed a test from the chemist. We ran to the town toilets where I unpeeled the test, read the instructions, and then peed on the stick. Then it was waiting time. After a few minutes two strong lines appeared. Checking the instructions, I turned to Kristy. "I'm pregnant."

My head swam. Yes, this was something we had wanted but not yet, not now, I still had two months left of college and had been offered a job through the nursery that I did placement days with through the college. How could I be pregnant? I took my pills and never missed a single one. Then it hit me… I was sick, really sick, that one night of drinking had led to this moment. Now I had to tell my mum and Scott. I was terrified as I made my way to Superdrug where my mum worked. She took one look at me and frowned. "What's wrong?" she asked.

I couldn't get the words out. I thought she was going to be so disappointed in me, I was only eighteen, yes I was working, and had been with Scott five years at that point, but she had me young. She had me on her seventeenth birthday. I just looked at her waiting for the shouts. "Don't be mad, Mum," I pleaded, bursting into tears.

She came out from behind the till and threw her arms around me. "Mad? Why would I be mad? You are an adult, Vikki! Have you told Scott?" *Shit, I've got to ring Scott now!*

After kissing my mum, I turned to Kristy. "That wasn't so bad!" We went outside and I pulled out my phone, dialling his number.

"Hello?" he said.

"Scott, it's me. I just did a pregnancy test… and it's positive, I'm pregnant." Then I had to hold the phone away from my ear as all I could hear was shouting and whooping. "Scott, Scott, listen to me, it might be wrong; in fact, it probably *is*, so don't go telling anyone until I go to my doctors and get it confirmed, OK?"More screaming and shouting.

"Yes! Tom, pregnant, Vikki is pregnant! I know great, eh?! OK, you can't walk back from the town, wait for me and I will come and pick you up!" I looked at Kristy who could hear the whole conversation; in fact, I was sure the whole of Letchworth could at this point.

"I can walk, I'm only pregnant," I replied. Kristy was holding back her giggles at this point.

"Right listen, I'm coming to get you, where are you? Your dad just said we are celebrating tonight with a BBQ. Don't move, I'm on my way. Where are you again?"

"I'm outside Superdrug. I will see you soon but, Scott, please don't tell anyone else yet, promise me, as I need to get it confirmed."

"Yeah I won't say a thing. See you soon."

I looked at Kristy. "Well he's happy!" I said.

Scott pulled up five minutes later beaming that great big smile of his as I got in the car. "I'm so happy I was shouting all the way here out of the window! I saw my friend and told him."

I looked at him "You didn't! I said not to say anything!"

Scott beamed back at me. "Look, if the test says you are, then you are!" We dropped Kristy home and went back to my mum's house. My dad was equally over the moon and gave me a huge hug. We waited for my mum to come home and we celebrated, just us and my brothers.

I did six more tests after that day, I even went into the chemist and did a urine sample – they all came back positive, but I didn't truly believe it until my doctor confirmed it. *Wow I'm going to be a Mum,* I thought.

The next few months sailed by; it was an easy pregnancy, no sickness, I actually felt great - but I couldn't shake off the nagging doubt in my mind that something wasn't right. I voiced my concerns to Scott on a few occasions, but he told me not to be silly and said I was just worried because I was a first time mum, and as a few friends had had miscarriages lately it was bound to affect me. I wanted to believe him but a little nagging voice just wouldn't leave my head. Every time I went to the toilet I checked for blood. In the end I went to the doctor who said there was no reason for me to lose the baby, I was passed the three month stage and would be due a scan soon. I tried to relax.

My scan date rolled around, I couldn't wait to see my baby and of course to find out what sex the baby was so I could buy pink or blue - lemons and creams didn't appeal to me! The pregnancy was still going well at this point, but I could not stand the smell of chip shop chips, I would be violently sick if I smelt it. It got to the point where I would have to strategically plan my route so I didn't have to walk pass one! At this point, I had left college and gained a BTEC diploma in childhood studies. I walked straight out of college and into my dream job – a nursery nurse, looking after three to five year olds.

Scott and I walked into the scan room hand in hand; I rolled up my top and stared at the grainy screen as the sonographer smeared some jelly on my tummy. I turned to Scott and grinned. We were going to see our baby! There it was - little button nose and pouty lips! The image of Scott's profile. We watched in awe as our baby moved around on the screen.

"Can we find out the sex today, please?" I asked.

"Of course." The sonographer smiled and carried on. Measurements were taken, notes written, and then she turned to me. "I'm afraid the baby has its bum down and legs crossed so I can't see the sex, but you have a healthy baby, no concerns at all. Your due date is the 29th January 2002."

I looked at Scott and relief washed over me. He was right, nothing was wrong, our baby was fine! But I was gutted we didn't know what we were having, the waiting was going to be torture!

I got to about seven months pregnant when I decided I just couldn't wait any longer to find out the sex of the baby, I desperately needed to know! After flicking through my baby magazines I came across an advert for a private scan - £90 for lots of detailed scan pictures and a video with the music of your choice playing in the background of the scan.

I gave Scott my puppy eyed look. "Can I book this? Please?"

The thing with Scott is he can never say no to me, I only have to mention something and he will go out of his way to make sure I get it."Of course! Book it!" I managed to get an appointment for a Saturday which was perfect as my dad and Scott (who worked together at a cleaning firm) had that day off.

It was decided that my dad would drive us in his work van and my mum would also come as she wanted to see her grandchild. Scott had chosen the song 'When You Say Nothing At All' by Ronan Keating would be played in the background of the scan. After an hour driving we walked excitedly up the cobbled streets, and into the little building. I gave my name and took a seat. I was so excited, today was the day we would find out what colour scheme we could go with!

When we were called into a room, I handed over the CD and lay down, rolling up my top. The sonographer and I exchanged pleasantries while she squirted the jelly onto my tummy, then the screen came alive with the image of my baby. The song played in the background...

*The smile on your face lets me know that you need me. There's a truth in your eyes saying you'll never leave me. The touch of your hand says you'll catch me wherever I fall. You say it best when you say nothing at all .*Ronan Keating sang quietly.

The baby moved its hand and kind of waved, then turned its head away from the scan and kicked its little legs. I was amazed that we had created this little bundle of gorgeousness! My parents grinned and Scott squeezed my hand.

"OK, would you like to know the sex?"

"Yes!"We all replied at once.

She smiled and carried on, zooming into the picture. "It's a boy."

A boy! We all smiled and Scott's eyes welled with tears. A little boy - now I had to fight Scott over names!

We carried on watching the screen and listening to the music when all of a sudden the music stopped and the lady placed the scanner down. She sat down and looked me in the eye. "I'm sorry, but there is something really wrong with your baby's heart. I have never seen this before."

I looked at Scott as the colour drained from his face. My heart started to race and my head screamed, 'I told you so! I told you!'

That was when the shouting began. My mum and dad were firing off questions and Scott was angry. I just lay there blank.

"What do you mean something is seriously wrong?! You need to get someone in here to look!" Scott screamed desperately.

"I'm sorry but I am not trained, I don't know what I have seen, I just know I haven't seen it before. You need to go straight to the hospital. I will print these pictures of his heart for you to take."

I yanked down my top and grabbed the scan pictures and video, just wanting to get straight to the hospital. We made our way downstairs in a state of shock. Around us, pregnant women filled the waiting room, all smiles. I walked up to the desk, paid and left. By the time we got to the van my mum was crying and my dad was shouting about how unprofessional she was with the way she told us. I was blank, numb, and void of all emotion. We got to the van and Scott just broke, he sobbed and sobbed, and then I cried as we held each other.

The drive to the hospital was the longest hour of our lives. We sat in silent shock. I gripped Scott's hand tightly as my parents gave each other the odd worried glance. When we arrived at the hospital, I explained to the lady behind the desk that we needed a scan as soon as we could because something was wrong with my baby's heart.

"I'm sorry, we don't scan on weekends. No one is available, please come back Monday."

I actually couldn't believe my ears. Come back Monday?! More shouting. My dad and Scott were asking why there wasn't anyone available to scan at the weekend. More waiting. This would become a very regular thing in our lives from that day on.

That weekend I was a wreck. By this time we were living at a hostel in Hitchin because the flat would no way accommodate the three of us. The hostel was nice, we were lucky as we had the whole ground floor of a converted Victorian house. We had our own kitchen, bathroom, front room, bedroom, storage room, and a little garden. Everyone above us had to share a kitchen and bathroom, so I felt very lucky and was happy there.

I tortured myself those two days of waiting. I couldn't eat sleep or function properly. Every time I closed my eyes I imagined the little boy I had grown to love so much, and wondered if his heart was struggling to work or if it would stop beating at any moment. Scott withdrew into himself too, keeping himself busy. We both avoided talking about it.

When Monday finally rolled around, we went straight back to the hospital where I was taken for a scan. Instead of being excited, my whole body pulsated with fear. What would they find? What if he had died?

13

The sonographer turned to me. "I can see something in the heart but our scanner is not picking it up clearly. We need to transfer you to Guy's Hospital to have a detailed heart scan."

The appointment was made for two weeks' time. More waiting. I could have screamed with frustration but what could we do? We *had* to wait. So life dragged by slowly - Scott went to work and so did I. The girls at work knew I was having a private scan as it was all I had talked about so was eager to see the scan pictures and video. I took them in, they all circled around me and looked at the black and white images of my baby's feet, his hands and his little face. Then we went into the quiet room and put the video into the machine, they all got excited, watching my baby waving, moving and swimming around the screen.

I turned away. I couldn't bear to see it, or hear that song again. It actually took me along long time to be able to hear that song without welling up. To this day I have only ever watched the scan video once; it hurts too much and brings back to many painful memories. Plastering on a smile, I didn't tell them anything about the heart or scare. I wasn't ready to talk about it, I was still in shock. Work kept me sane for those two weeks.

The day finally came and we made our way to Guy's Hospital in London. We arrived early, but my mum, Scott and I were ushered through and seen immediately. The doctor explained he was a heart specialist and I would be having a detailed scan which would take up to an hour, I was not to move

14

and not to talk until he had looked at the scan himself afterwards.

I lay down and began the routine of rolling up my top, the screen was turned on but I turned my face away. I no longer enjoyed scans; they were scary and just made me feel anxious. I saw the colours swirling, different colours lit up the different parts of our baby's heart. I could hear the soft thump thump of the heart beating, which still makes me feel sick to this day. I only took small glances but could see measuring and zooming in, I knew something had been found and I bit my lip hard to stop the tears falling. Finally it was over, and we were told to wait in a room while they analysed the scan results.

When consultant walked in and sat down I could tell by his face something was wrong. "I have found three lumps in your baby's heart which are rhabdomyomas and are benign tumours of strained muscle. Rhabdomyomas are usually linked to the condition Tuberous Sclerosis which your son has a high chance of having, but it can be diagnosed at the birth."

I stared at him in shock. I had no idea what this condition was, but I knew it didn't sound good. My mum promptly burst into floods of tears and shouted, "Why us? What next? What did we ever do?"

Scott just stared ahead.

The specialist continued talking. "We will send you for genetic testing and counselling. In the meantime, here is some information on Tuberous Sclerosis." He handed me a black and white sheet but it contained barely any writing or information.

"What is Tuberous Sclerosis?" I asked.

He looked at my mum, who had now composed herself, then to Scott and finally back to me. "It is a condition that causes benign tumours to grow in the brain and other vital organs such as the kidneys, heart, lungs eyes and skin. It can cause learning difficulties seizures and autism, along with other disorders."

I took the sheet from him and, for that moment, pushed all of the worries aside. Things like this don't happen to people like us, I was young fit and healthy, I was eighteen! Eighteen year olds do not have disabled children. We would be fine, our baby would be fine. I was kidding myself.

The next couple of months passed in a haze of preparing for our arrival. The wardrobes and cot were put up, the clothes washed, the steriliser unpacked and the pram was on order. I didn't tell anyone about the chance of our son having TS, I pushed it to the back of my mind. Scott had the same attitude, he would be fine he was strong. After much disagreement we finally agreed on the name Kai which I read had the meaning strong, unbreakable and was short for Kaiden, which had the meaning survivor. Appointments were sent for us to see the genetics counsellor in Luton and, as usual, my mum wanted to come with us.

That week I had hardly done much washing as I was busy with washing Kai's bits and getting things ready, so unknown to me, Scott had no pants, but he managed to find a small pair he just about squeezed into. We travelled to Luton and our name was called, we were asked for one of us to come into the room at a time, so I went first. I was asked lots of questions such as, was there a history of seizures in the family? Tumours, Kidney problems? I was then asked to get undressed down to my underwear so she could shine a special light over my body to see if I had the tell-tale white patches that comes with TS - they wanted to rule out me or Scott having the condition as it can be genetic or just a one off random occurrence. The lights were turned off and a hand held strobe type light was run over my body from head to toe. Finally, the lights went back on.

"I'm pleased to say you don't have the white patches. I will refer you for blood tests and also check your husband. But I have to ask, what would you like to do?"

I stared at her not understanding the question. "Like to do?"

She smiled at me sympathetically and continued, "Would you like to continue with the pregnancy? You have options."

I stared at her, horrified. I had felt this baby move and seen his little face on the screen, I had bonded with and named this baby. "Of course I want to keep him!"

She smiled and led me to the door, it was now Scott's turn. My mum and I sat and waited, chatting about how it was a good sign I had no white patches and no history of any of the symptoms in our family - only epilepsy on Scott's side with his granddad.

Suddenly, Scott came bursting out of the door bright red and eager to leave. "Let's go now!"

I looked at him in panic. "Why? Did they find something? Is everything OK?"

He lead us down the corridor and whispered, "I didn't know she was going to ask me to strip, if I did I would have found some decent pants! The ones I have on are too small and my balls are hanging out!"

I looked at my mum and we tried to hide our giggles.

Scott continued, "As soon as I realised she wanted me to strip I went bright red, pulled my top off and trousers and socks. When she bent down with the light to run it over my body, my balls were hanging out of the side of my pants! She noticed as well as she was trying not to laugh. I've never been so embarrassed in my life!"

All three of us collapsed into a fit of giggles. I was never going to let him live this one down!

MEETING KAI

The rest of the pregnancy went well.I was getting very bad heartburn which kept me awake a lot at night, so I was relieved when I finally went on maternity leave. I took the opportunity to lounge in bed and watch TV, read and visit my mum most days. I also passed my driving test at eight months pregnant, which gave me the freedom to do what I wanted as Scott was working longer hours. It was over at my parent's that I started to look up Tuberous Sclerosis on the computer. I found only a few stories and avoided the medical jargon as it all seemed to be doom and gloom. I found a few stories of hope and seemed to calm myself with thoughts of 'well if as bad as it gets is epilepsy, I can deal with that' ...oh, how my young mind worked!

After lots of appointments to talk through my labour and the future, it was decided that the best place to have Kai would be at Guy's Hospital in

London because they needed to keep an eye on the rhbdomyomas. They'd told me there were two small ones and a large one, they were concerned that they could block a vent in his heart from closing, which can happen after birth.

I was given the date of 20th January 2002 to meet my little boy. This was also Scott's granddad's birthday, who we were very close to, so it seemed apt. We had bloods and family history appointments and another scan. Everything was ready for the birth, we just had to wait. Christmas came and went and I wondered how much more room the baby needed; I'd already gone from a size 8 up to a 14, which was all bump! We celebrated New Year at my mum's house. My dad and Scott had a few drinks; we saw midnight come and go and then we went to bed. I realised we had left our mobile phones at home but didn't think that would be a problem. We arrived home the next day around lunchtime and I ached so went for a soak. Scott realised we had lots of missed calls on our phones from his mum and brother so went to give them a call to wish them happy New Year. When I got out of the bath and walked into the bedroom, I found Scott sitting on the bed, sobbing.

"He's gone, my granddad has died."

We were crushed as we were close to him and gutted he wouldn't get to meet our baby. I had a horrible feeling he would pass before Kai's birth because the previous month we had gone to visit him in hospital and he was very pale and groaning with pain. When Scott and everyone left the room he'd held onto my hand and said, "Take care of you and the baby."

I'd looked at him and smiled. "You will meet him soon granddad!" He just kept hold of my hand and looked at me and I knew. I never told Scott about that moment as I didn't think he could cope with much more.

The funeral was tough and I didn't think I could cry as much as I did although I tried my hardest to stay strong for Scott. I was due to be induced in a few days' time and was ready to pop. We decided to add the names John Dean as Kai's middle name as Dean was Scott's middle name and John was granddad's name. Kai John Dean Hammond had a little ring to it. I liked it.

The night before my induction we packed the car, baby bag, nappies, wipes, clothes, blankets, car seat, my things and a bag for Scott as we were to stay in hospital for a while, depending on how Kai was once he finally arrived. All of my family lived two minutes away from Guy's Hospital, as that was where I was born and grew up so it was nice that I would get to see my nanny Pat, who I was closer to than anyone, my granddad Terry, my great Nan Violet and my biological father, Darren and my step mum, Terri, my half-brothers and my sisters Charlie, Katie, Georgia and Harry (Lily-Rose would be born the year later).Once packed I had a nice bath and felt Kai moving and kicking as I had a long soak. I lay in that water and got quite emotional. This is the last time I will feel this. We were due to meet Kai very soon! We couldn't sleep that night; we were full of nerves and excitement, worry and fear.

The next morning we got up early - 5am- and my dad came to collect us. We drove to London and looked for a cafe to have breakfast. We sat, freezing cold, in the cafe talking about anything and everything to pass the time away. I wasn't due at the hospital until ten but we had got there early to beat the rush-hour traffic. I kissed my dad who was going home and bringing my mum back the following day. Scott and I walked to my Nan's house, and sat chatting, all the time looking at the clock. Finally, it was time to leave. This was it, the moment we had been waiting for.

My stomach was in knots as we made the short walk to the hospital. As we arrived I got settled in a bed on the labour ward and had my observations done, blood pressure, urine sample, baby's heart rate, all those sort of things. I was told I would be given a pessary around tea time and to rest. As the day passed, I noticed little tightening's in my tummy but didn't really think much of it. When I was checked again, at teatime, in preparation for the pessary the nurse said, "Oh, you are having contractions." *Wow, I thought, if that's all they feel like I will be fine!*.

The pessary started to work and I could feel the contractions getting stronger and stronger with each minute that passed, as the night went on, I writhed and wriggled in pure agony. Watching other women leave to go to the delivery suite I wanted to scream. I was given gas and air and managed to cope, but by the morning I was distressed. A doctor came over to see how far dilated I was and I swear he had the biggest hands ever. I screamed at him never to come near me again. I was really embarrassed. Scott was trying to calm me down so I would let the doctor continue with his examination, but I crossed my legs and refused.

Deciding I wanted to go for a bath, I made Scott follow behind me, wheeling the gas canister along. The bath did little to ease the pain and by this point I was really struggling to cope so I was taken to the delivery suite. A really lovely, and very patient, midwife met me there. She was great with me and gave me an epidural which dulled the pain a little but I could still feel a lot of pain. By two o'clock my parents arrived and my mum was allowed in with Scott to watch the birth.

More hours went by and Scott, having not eaten all day, decided to go to McDonalds to grab a burger and I was too far gone to even care at this point and so he went to leave. As soon as he left the room, dreaming about how many burgers he could consume in ten minutes, the midwife shouted after him. "Quick there's no time the baby is coming now!"

To this day Scott swears it's because Kai heard the word McDonald's! And funny enough it is his favourite food ever.

Scott rushed back in the room with my mum running behind him. I was pushing with all my might but nothing was happening and I was at the point of screaming the place down. I had been contracting since the night before so it was coming up to twenty two hours of pain!

I was so delirious with pain that when the midwife said, "I need to cut you to get the baby out."

I shouted "NO!"

Scott, by this point, just wanted to meet his little boy and said over me, "She said yes!" I shot him a dagger and then all of a sudden I felt a lot of pressure and then the pain was gone.

Scott told me later that Kai come flying out as soon as the cut was made and the midwife just about managed to catch him! I heard a little cry and my baby was being taken off to be cleaned up; finally, they handed him to me wrapped in a blanket. I will never forget that moment as long as I live. Staring up at me was a perfect button nosed, blue eyed and blond haired little boy. He had big kissable lips, just like his daddy, and the same nose.

Scott lent over me and so did my mum and we all just cried - although Scott more than us! We had five minutes with him before he had to be taken down to the special care baby unit. Kai was born at 7.25pm on the 21st January 2002.Unwrapping the hospital blanket, I had a better look at my beautiful little bundle. He had perfect hands feet and his little tummy was moving up and down. I was just about to wrap him back up when I noticed two white patches on his arm (tell-tale signs of TS).

"He has white patches on his arm," I said to the midwife.

She took a look and said, "Oh, they could be birthmarks, we will have a look."

I handed him to her and thought they know what they are talking about and thought no more of it. The room filled with doctors, specialists and students and they congratulated us then wheeled him off with Scott following behind them.

My dad came bursting in the room. "I missed it by five minutes! Every bloody traffic light was red on the way here!"

Scott fed Kai his first bottle and sat and held his hand through the plastic incubator that was to be his little home those next few days. He came back and relayed his information. "He's perfect! I fed him his bottle, his skin is so soft! Thank you so much for giving me a son!"

After I was stitched and cleaned up, my mum and dad said their goodbyes as they had to travel the two hours back to Hertfordshire. "We will be back tomorrow. I'm so proud of you. I love you," my mum said, kissing me goodbye.

Scott wheeled me to see Kai on the SCBU ward. As I walked in I saw very poorly babies, tiny babies, and babies with tubes and wires covering every inch of them. Then I saw Kai. He was three times the size of them and healthy and at that moment I felt *so* thankful. He was a good weight–8lbs– even though he was eight days early. Scott wheeled me over and we sat and stared in wonder at this little life we had created.

"He's perfect, just perfect," I said. The doctors explained he would be wired up to a machine and have bedside scans to check that the vent in his heart could close without the tumour blocking it and causing problems (which usually happened around day 3-5). So we just had to wait and see.

A few days later, I saw an incubator empty. "Where's the baby from that incubator?" I asked a nurse.

"He sadly passed away," He replied. My heart broke for that family.

The next few days were a flurry of visitors. Everyone wanted to meet our new baby. The room was filled with balloons, teddies and cards all screaming out 'It's a boy!' The next few days we spent getting to know our son. We were allowed to feed him, bath him, and hold him. Then, on day four, we were told we could have him in our room on the ward. His heart was fine and the tumour wasn't obstructing the vent after all! We could have burst with happiness and relished in that night, even when he woke us every two hours for a bottle we were still beaming in the morning.

After final tests we were told we could go home. We were to come back in a few months' time to have another scan to make sure that the tumours didn't grow. No TS was mentioned so we went to pack our bags, ecstatic that we could finally go home and be a family. Scott drove so slowly that it took us double the time to get home and every speed bump he crawled over - his precious son was in the car, he was taking no risks! We drove straight to Scott's Aunt Sheila's house to show him off to his brothers and family. As soon as we got home that night we were exhausted and went straight to bed.

The phone calls and texts were all made the next morning, letting everyone know we had just had our baby. Cards arrived, presents, balloons and visitors. When Kai was two days old my biological father, Darren phoned. "We didn't want to tell you and upset you as you had just had Kai but your nanny Violet passed away."

I was hurt and angry, especially when I found out Scott knew but had been told to keep it from me. Though, once I had calmed down, I realised why it was kept from me, she had died the same night Kai came into the world.

Those next few weeks were a blur of nappy changing, bottle making, feeding and rocking. It was a real achievement if I managed to get dressed during the day! Once Scott went back to work we got ourselves into a little routine that worked for us and managed to start leaving the house. I spent a lot of time at my mum's, driving us to the town or sitting and chatting, visiting work and letting the children hold the baby they were forever asking questions about.

Kai was a good baby, rarely cried, loved his bottles, and was very content to just sit in his bouncy chair or lay kicking his legs on the play mat. One day I was at my mum's with Scott and we were just getting ready to leave when she picked up Kai for a cuddle. As she nuzzled into his cheek she screamed, "He's not breathing, Kai's not breathing!"

Scott ran over and grabbed him, holding him at arm's length to take a look at him. Kai stared back at us smiling, "He's fine, Mum! He's OK! "

She was shook up and wiped her tears once she saw he was fine. We talked about it on the way home and couldn't understand why my mum thought Kai wasn't breathing, but it soon became abundantly clear.

SOMETHING IS WRONG

One day not too long after the visit to my mum's, I was feeding Kai his baby rice in his bouncy chair when he suddenly arched his back and grimaced, throwing his arms in the air and making little noises. The only way I can describe it is when a new-born is picked up and put down and they pull that face, arms in the air - like the startle reflex. As soon as it started, though, it stopped, so I didn't think that much of it. The next day Kai screamed all day and all night, which was extremely out of character. Concerned, we checked his temperature, nappy, if he was too hot or too cold, tummy ache or just tired. Nothing appeared to be wrong, yet he continued to cry. He also did the 'arms up' thing again, so we took him to the doctor. I explained he did the weird face, arms up, back arched and how he had changed from happy to crying all day and night. The doctor diagnosed it as colic and said to give him gripe water.

The next day was the same.

Still unhappy, I called Scott from work and we took him to our local hospital A&E. The doctors listened and fully examined him and, again, I was told it was colic.

The next day Kai wasn't too bad, he seemed happier, which was good as we had just been given a two bedroom flat in Letchworth by the council; luckily though, we had managed to exchange it straight away with Scott's childhood home where his aunt lived alone in a three bedroom house with a big garden. It had been in the family for well over sixty years. It was too much work for his aunt to upkeep as she worked full time and was getting on in age, so the ground floor flat next to the shops we had just been assigned was perfect for her! The downside was we had just a few days to move us into the house and move his aunt out of the house and into the flat!

Later that day, as I was dressing Kai for bed he had another episode, but this time he looked in a pure panic and fearful with no response during it. He then did it again as we were putting him the car to take him back to the hospital. I was in a real state at this point and rushed him through the doors of the accident and emergency. He was again diagnosed with colic even after we went through his birth and all of our history with them. I knew it was something more but I had been told three times in one week it was colic so we took him home. I spoke to my step mum that night and expressed my concerns to her.

"If you are not happy, Vikki, you need to take him back. You are his mum, you know him best."

So the following day, when he did it again, I took him straight back to the hospital. The nurses by this point were exasperated with me and I got the feeling I was annoying them! I was in a real state, sobbing as Kai lay screaming in his car seat with Scott trying to soothe him.

The nurse pulled the curtain around us. "Look you are clearly exhausted. You are a new mum with a demanding baby, this screaming he is doing is for attention." And with that she picked him up and he calmed down. "See, he just wants you. I think you need a break. Give him to your mum for a few days and rest. He has colic; he'll grow out of it."

I felt like screaming at her that something was wrong with him, I could feel it in my gut - it was the same feeling as when he was inside me. I just knew this wasn't colic, it was something more, but I was beat down, tired and no match for a mature nurse. I figured that perhaps she was right, perhaps it was me and it was in my head.

Just as I picked him up to leave I really felt despair and anger. "No one is listening to us," I said to Scott. "Why won't they listen?"I was just about to walk out of the double doors when Kai suddenly stiffened again, arms raised, grimaced face and arched back. I ran back and grabbed a passing doctor and handed Kai over to him. "Look! This is what he does!" I shouted.

The doctor took one look at Kai and said, "He's having a seizure!" and ran into a room with Kai in his arms.

The next two hours are a still a blur to this day. I was sobbing, yet Scott was trying to stay calm while the doctors fired questions at us. It was then decided that he needed a lumber puncture to rule out meningitis. We were not allowed into the room with him while this procedure was carried out because it was distressing to witness. So I sat six doors away sobbing into my hands. I knew that was one of the most painful procedures you can have and my four-month-old baby was going to be having one done alone. I could hear his screams all those doors away and just sat with my fingers in my ears, sobbing, trying to block out the sound.

As soon as I was handed back my baby I cuddled him to me closely and my silent tears fell onto his head. The doctors explained that Kai would need more tests and instructed we were to stay the night, but Scott had to go home. Of course, he didn't want to leave but there was no other choice. We *had* to move out the following day or would have to pay an extra week of rent on the house, and we just didn't have the money for that. I spent the night tossing and turning, unable to sleep and jumping at every murmur Kai made.

The following day we were blue-lighted to Addenbrookes Hospital in Cambridge for more tests. It happened so suddenly that I didn't even have the chance to tell Scott until we were nearly there, but when we pulled up he was there waiting. We settled into the ward and doctors came and went, asking question after question and taking observations and blood of Kai's. Scott had to leave after a couple of hours as he had to get the packing and moving started for the following day.

"I'll see you tomorrow night," he said, kissing our heads. He has since told me that it felt like it killed him having to leave us there alone, but there was simply no other choice. We just couldn't afford two weeks rent.

The ward was nice and clean and I had a bed next to Kai's cot, a chair and a bedside phone which I made full use of ringing my mum, my dad's and Scott's family. I didn't phone my nan at that point because I didn't want to alarm her, she was just going through treatment for breast cancer that she had been battling for the past five years. I couldn't eat that night, I just sat staring at my boy and wondering what was going to happen, I didn't sleep much either my head just wouldn't shut off.

The following day I managed to speak to a rushed Scott who had just hours to get everything sorted and wanted to be back at the hospital with us by the evening. I managed to grab a paper and magazine and just sat passing the time away when Kai was sleeping by reading. The curtain was pulled back just as I was standing over Kai, who I had just lay down for his nap.

"Hi, I'm Doctor Smith Please sit down." I looked at his face and watched him pull the curtain around us, I knew when you were told to sit down it was bad news. I sat down. "We have run some tests on Kai and we believe he has the condition Tuberous Sclerosis."

I looked at the doctor sitting, legs crossed and I just felt the last few months' worth of anger rising to the top of my head. "You are wrong,"

I said. "We were sent home from Guy's Hospital. He was fine, his hearts fine!"

"I'm afraid he does have Tuberous Sclerosis, Miss Chambers. Is there someone I can call who you would like here to support you?"

I stood up and just started screaming, "You're wrong. You're wrong! Why are you lying to me?" He tried to calm me down but all of the emotion just flooded out of me. "Get out!! Get out! You are lying!!"

The doctor didn't know where to look and swiftly left as I pulled the curtain back for him. Then I fell. I fell to the floor and I sobbed and sobbed until I couldn't cry any more. *Not him, not my baby, not us. This doesn't happen to people like us...does it?*

I picked up the phone, needing to hear my nan's voice, but when she answered I just broke down. I couldn't get my words out, they were lodged in my throat. She caught bits and pieces of it and started to cry with me, I had never heard my nan cry and it brought me back to reality. I managed to compose myself.

"They are saying he has it, Nan, but they are wrong!"

I could hear silent crying. "Vikki, listen to me where's Scott? Who is with you? Have you eaten?"

I had decided to wait until Scott came into the hospital to tell him as I didn't want him upset driving to us. "Scott's moving all our stuff, Nan. I'm on my own. No, I haven't eaten; I'm not hungry."

My nan's tone changed as she spoke again. "Listen to me, you are no good in this state. Please eat something; Kai needs you. I wish I could come and be with you, Vikki, I really do."

"I'm not hungry, Nan, I can't eat. I wish you could be here, too." That was impossible though, with her treatment she was undergoing, she couldn't risk coming to the hospital in case she picked up an infection.

After she had calmed me down as much as she could I phoned my Mum, and my biological dad, Darren and told them the news. Now I had to wait for Scott to arrive.

Scott and I cried together that night, telling each other what we both thought the other wanted to hear. 'He will be fine. We can cope with seizures, that's the worst it will be, and people live with epilepsy and still lead a normal life.'

We had to stay strong, we would get through this, we would get through this together.

DENIAL

Kai was prescribed vigabatrin sachets to control his epilepsy - we were to mix the sachet with sterile water and give it to him via a sterilised syringe. It was a strong drug and one they hoped, if any, would work. It came with side effects, though, so he was only to be on it a few months because prolonged usage could possibly affect his vision.

After a few days, we were discharged and given in depth instructions on how to deal with seizures and when to worry etc. Together, the three of us went back to our new home. It needed a lot of work; literally every single room needed gutting and starting again. It was a big project but I knew Scott could handle it – and I was correct. He started on Kai's room first, painting it a nice lemon colour with Winnie The Pooh murals on the walls, pairing it with matching curtains. We filled the room with toys and a cot ready for him to go into when he outgrew his Moses basket.

I didn't tell anyone about Kai's diagnosis those first few months. I didn't want the sympathy stares and the pity that came with things like this. I told close family, of course, and we all had the same attitude: Kai would be fine, we could cope with epilepsy.

Kai continued to have 'infantile spasms' as they are referred to, he would have as many as ten a day, lasting a couple of minutes each. Over time, he just got on with it and didn't even cry after an episode. The next few months were filled with hospital appointments, genetics appointments, plus consultant and doctor appointments. Because of my training and qualification in childcare, I began to notice that Kai wasn't reaching his milestones. He could roll over and would smile, but had trouble looking into my eyes and wasn't attempting to sit up or crawl. Also, around this time, he began to have other types of seizures: he would stare blankly ahead and the hairs on his head would stand up, he was also doing a very unusual laugh and one side of his mouth would smile while he stared ahead. The doctors explained these were different types of seizures and wanted to take him off of the vigabatrin as his time limit on it was up and wanted to try him with a few months course of steroids.

Kai was seven months old when he went onto steroids. He seemed to change overnight, gaining weight over a period of a couple of short weeks, and crying more than usual. If he wasn't eating his lunch or having a bottle or sleeping, he would cry day and night. I was up and down so much that I was exhausted both mentally and physically. Nothing seemed to soothe him, he just screamed, and most nights I sat up with him crying along with him. As it became more obvious he was very behind from other babies, Scott and I began to argue. We were taking it out on each other, both tired and both in denial. One of us would ask the 'what if' question and the other would reassure, and then we would reverse roles. It was an extremely tiring and emotionally draining time.

Kai would never hold toys, he would throw them not bothering to explore, and if I sat him up he would flop back down again. When he went for his eight month check at the health visitors he failed every single thing. With each cross on the chart, my heart sank. There it was in black and white, my son was behind so there was no denying it now.

I think one of the first things a parent with a child with special needs feels is denial; when you first hold your new-born baby the first thing you have is hope. Hope that they do well in life, that they achieve all they can and they will progress with each milestone. You never imagine a life with a child with special needs, the expectations we have for our children are strong and so we dismiss any negative signs that something could be wrong or milestones are not met. And so we repress those feeling to protect ourselves. Only time can break this feeling of denial, but that time can be months, years or an event that you can't ignore, something will always come along to break the protective barrier that you put up and the walls to come crashing down. We would learn the hard way.

To have something to look forward to, Scott and I decided we would get married the following year, which left only a few months to prepare! We wanted June 1st as this was the date we got together, but had to have 31st May instead because our preferred date fell on a Sunday. After setting the date, I got planning. I had control and choice of everything – Scott had simply said, 'book what you want tell me the details and I'll show up!' Men!

MILESTONES

Milestones to a parent with special needs are like red flags. They simply show us how much our child is behind and what they *should* be doing compared to the average child. Milestones hurt, that's the truth of it. They're set in stone, are the guidelines and ages of what your child should be doing by this stage. When your child doesn't meet them it hurts, it really does. It leaves fear in our heart and we feel helpless lost and concerned. And then there is always the 'what ifs'? What if my child never sits up? What if he never crawls or walks or never says the words Mum and Dad? We torture ourselves, which is why when a milestone *is* met… no matter how small it may seem to you, it is big news to us! It fills our heart with hope and allows us to carry on the fight through our child. Which is why, when Kai first said the word Mum I cried pure tears of joy. I was standing in the kitchen cooking late one night and had just put Kai to bed, I could hear him over the monitor as clear as day "Mum, Mum, Mum!" I ran upstairs as fast as my legs could carry me and hugged him tightly.

Then at ten months, Kai was taken off the steroids and was actually seizure free for the next couple of months - which gave him time to learn a new thing…he sat up! With lots of support and cushions around him, he sat up and I wanted to scream from the roof tops!! He did it; my boy was proving us all wrong!

For the next few weeks we couldn't leave Kai sitting up on his own, because he would fall forward and hit his face on the floor – one time he even put his tooth through his lip. Kai never crawled, but he did learn to bum shuffle. He had his own unique way of dragging and rolling himself across the floor. His next word was Dad and Scott was absolutely over the moon! Every other week he would do something small that just took my breath away, hold a toy for longer than a second and place it in his mouth, or try to roll out of the room. Each milestone, however late it was, was a blessing and it really gave us some hope that things would be OK.

Despite everything, Kai was a very happy baby. He loved his grandmother, and demonstrated this by shouting 'Nan Nan' - not in the right context, but he said it and, to me, that was enough. He loved his Bob the Builder phone, he used to smash the buttons with the yellow receiver over and over again. He enjoyed music especially The Fimbles theme tune! He loved his food - shepherd's pie and a roast was his favourite. He had this ability to suck anyone he met into him without communicating, he just has a good aura and vibe about him. He loved bath time this was his favourite time of day and would giggle as he splashed.

As many dark days as we had had with Kai his strength and infectious happiness would cast them aside. Yes, he wasn't meeting the milestones when he should have been, and this became blatantly obvious around any child his age which was what would send daggers through my heart. They were standing pointing and cuddling their mum babbling and sitting with toys, trying to work them out or exploring their surroundings. Then there was Kai, flapping his hands and holding his hand in front of his face and looking at it in wonder over and over again. He was screeching and stuck in his own little world, ignoring toys and paying no interest in any of his surroundings.

Then I would notice the pity looks, and I knew they knew. My son was different, there was no denying it, it was plain for anyone to see but for now denial suited me just fine. Until the night that changed me.

THE NIGHT THAT CHANGED ME

It was a year to the day that Scott's Granddad had passed away and we decided it was still too raw to celebrate New Year so we had a quiet one and even went to bed before the clock struck midnight. On New Year's Day we went to Scott's uncles house for little get-together to remember granddad. I was so proud watching Kai sitting up alone with no cushions to support him, and stuffing his face with whatever he could get people to hand to him by charming them.

We went home happy and full. The next day was uneventful we spent the day stripping walls and looking at paint colours. Kai was his usual happy cheerful self; we even went around the shops and managed to grab a few bargains. Seven o'clock came around and I put Kai to bed in his new bargain pyjamas, kissing his chubby hand as I lay him down. Scott decided to go to his brother's house to borrow some DVDs as there was nothing much on TV. I tidied up for a bit and then decided to go and run a bath. As I turned the taps on I had a very strong feeling to go and check on Kai. It was the strangest experience I have ever had and I can't explain it even to this day. I shocked myself and couldn't shake off the feeling, and then it came to me, a voice in my head: *Go and check on Kai, now.* That's what it was, a voice, someone was telling me to go and check on my son, it was insistent. I had never really thought much of spirits and God, but that night changed all of that.

I turned the taps off and walked up the stairs. With each step the voice got louder and more urgent, as I started to sprint I already knew what I was going to find, I could see it as an image in my head. I swung the door open, heart racing, and ran to Kai's cot. From this point on it was almost as if I were watching it from out of my body, like I was above myself.

Kai was lying in his cot and his lips were blue, he was making a little grunting sound but no breath was leaving his body. Sick covered the cot and was smeared all over his cheeks and new pyjamas. It was at this point that I snapped back into myself. Picking up Kai, I ran as fast as I could, screaming down the stairs. All of my first aid training went out of the window; I had no idea what to do. I screamed and screamed, rolling him onto his side as I grabbed my phone. I rang for an ambulance, screaming that my son wasn't breathing, please, please hurry, please come. I shouted my address and didn't wait to listen to the response, I just threw the phone.

They say when a mother loses a child they howl like a wounded animal, it is a distinctive howl, and I could hear the howl leaving my throat as I sobbed over Kai just willing him to breathe. Just then the door knocked and I ran, Kai in my arms, to the door. It was my neighbour, Alan, his son and his son's friend. The way they were standing there I think they thought I was being murdered! I screamed that Kai wasn't breathing, that he was dead.

Immediately, Alan took Kai off me and ran into the kitchen. I moved to follow but was stopped by Adam and Ben who sat me down. "Stay here, you don't need to see what's happening."

I was rocking back and forth on the sofa, thoughts flashed through my mind. *He's dead, what is the quickest way I can be with him?* I planned my death –I would take my car and crash into a wall. I couldn't live with pain like this, not without my boy. I felt desperate to stop this pain; I couldn't imagine a life without Kai in it. I could hardly breathe, thoughts were flashing through my mind. How had everything changed so quickly? He'd been fine earlier, so what had I missed or done wrong? I had never experienced such a raw feeling of utter desperation, I felt helpless. I sat waiting trying to stop the howl that kept coming from my body, trying to rock the pain away.

Ben ran out to wait for the ambulance and Alan walked back through carrying Kai. "He's breathing, Vikki, look. He had choked on his sick but I've unblocked it from his airways. He is breathing."

I took Kai from him and hugged him tight, he was so hot to touch and was quite limp and unresponsive but he *was* breathing. When the ambulance arrived they took his temperature and found it was through the roof.

"He's convulsing," they said, and rushed him into the ambulance, and I ran to join him.

I will never be able to thank Alan enough for that night. He got my baby breathing again and later became a Godparent to Kai. As did his wife, Julie.

Scott, I later learned, had arrived home to see police and ambulances blocking the drive and he got out and ran into the house, where Alan explained what had happened. He has so much regret over that night and blamed himself for a long time after for not being there. But how were we to know? An hour before Kai hadn't had so much as a sniffle.

Scott had arrived at the hospital just after we had and came running into the hospital. Kai was immediately whisked off and we were asked questions about his condition and how he had been lately. Once answered, they told us that Kai was still convulsing and we were to wait outside while they tried to stabilise him. We were hysterical. Scott rang his family and I rang mine and they all raced to the hospital. I hadn't smoked in years but that night I smoked and smoked until I was called back in. Kai was now stable. He had convulsed for almost an hour, but they didn't know the outcome of the seizure he had had. We were admitted to a ward and both slept on the floor next to Kai's cot. He was checked on throughout the night as I lay there staring at the ceiling.

He slept until around nine in the morning and as soon as he woke up I sprung out of the chair next to his bed. Kai looked at his hand, turned it around and staring at it as he often did and then said, "Dadda." My boy was back!

For breakfast, he downed two bottles and had some porridge; I was so excited I rang everyone to tell them he was fine there was no damage that I could see so far. Kai was transferred to Addenbrookes Hospital where they found he had a nasty virus, it had literally come on within minutes of putting him to bed and his temperature was so high that his little body convulsed, causing him to vomit which he had then choked on.

We spent a few days there with him as his temperature was still high and hard to keep down and he had now developed a very upset tummy. We had a swarm of visitors in those coming days. Kai was his usual happy self and had charmed all of the nurses with those big blue eyes of his. Night times were bad; I panicked at every little noise and couldn't erase the image of that night. It still haunts me to this day and I struggle to talk about it, I don't think I will ever come close to that feeling again. It was pure panic and fear, the thoughts that race through your mind when you are holding your child in your arms and they aren't breathing, I can't even begin to describe it. It was a physical pain straight through my heart and all I wanted was the pain to stop and to be with my boy – even if that meant being with him in death, I would have done it in a heartbeat.

I later found out that it had really affected Alan, my neighbour, for months afterwards - although he has never told me personally, his wife, Julie, told me that he found it hard to talk about. The night Kai nearly died Julie had also heard my screams as did her daughter and her niece and they stood cuddling on the doorstep praying to God that Kai would be OK. God listened that night. The experience brought me closer to my neighbours and to this day, we still share a bond.

That night changed me in so many ways. It made me realise how fragile life is, it also made me think deeper about the voice I had heard warning me. I had always had little psychic feelings, mainly with Kai, I had always known, right from when he was conceived, that something was wrong. But that voice was more than a gut instinct. To this day I still believe the voice was mine and Kai's guardian angel. It's easy to dismiss these sort of things if you are a non-believer, but when something like that happens to you there is no denying it. If I hadn't heard the voice, Kai would be dead. I also believe that the reason I knew what I was going to find walking up those stairs was visions. I still have them to this day but not as vivid as that night.

That night made me believe that God did exist and there is life after death. But the main thing that night had changed in me was denial, after that my denial vanished completely, I could no longer pretend he was like any other child. He was my perfect little boy but he was also very unwell and would always need me - which lead me onto the next phase parents with special needs go through… acceptance.

THE STAGES OF GRIEF

I believe that when you have a child with any kind of special need you go through a grief process, sometimes you go through them over and over again and not in any order either. The first thing I felt was denial. I guess it was a form of protection, kind of like: if I didn't accept it then it's not happening. It's easy to kid yourself that your child will be fine, that there has been some kind of mistake and they have got it wrong - he will show them all! It's only as time goes on and it becomes obvious that your child isn't hitting their milestones or showing behaviour that isn't considered the norm that it becomes a bit harder to deny.

The next stage I went through was isolation. I pushed away everyone I was close to that first year of Kai's life. I didn't see my friends, I pushed Scott away and I didn't leave the house much other than to visit my mum's or attend hospital appointments.

Being a mum of a special needs child is a very lonely world anyway but I didn't help myself. Looking back, I feel sad for that scared nineteen-year-old girl I once was. I'd avoided people so I didn't have to answer their questions which would mean I would have to accept TS and I wasn't ready to.

I then went through the bargaining stage, 'please God take this away from my son'. If only I had done things differently… Then you look for the smallest thing like: did eating that packed of peanuts do this? Did I do this to my child? Could I have done anything differently? Am I being punished? Bargaining then leads on to anger. I felt angry with the world, with God, and with the hospital for not diagnosing him at birth. They let me think Kai was OK and let me lead a nice normal life for a while, that left a bitter taste in my mouth. Why me? Why us? Why my baby? I hated seeing other children reaching up and cuddling their mum or pushing a car along the floor or walking, each time I saw any of these it left me feeling angry and cold. Anger is like a poison and it eats away at you, but it is a side effect of denial, it deflects our denial onto something else which builds up like a rage inside you.

The next stage for me was guilt. Did I do the right thing having Kai? Was it fair on him? Did I do this to him? Did I also have TS and had passed it to him? Why couldn't I accept he had this illness? All of these thoughts rush through your mind and you begin to blame yourself, you are his mum, so why can't you make him better? There are other stages you go through in the grief cycle, but the night that changed me lead me onto acceptance, the other stages I will come to later on.

Coming home from the hospital was bittersweet I was glad to be back but also absolutely petrified. For weeks after we got home I went to bed when Kai did, sleeping on the floor next to his cot. I checked his breathing and I panicked if he so much as got the sniffles. The beautiful pyjamas I had brought him now made me go straight back to that night so I threw them in the bin along with blankets and sheets that was in his cot. I wanted no reminders of that night.

Scott and I became closer again. We'd had a taster of how bad things could get and I hated Scott leaving for work now and he hated leaving me. I was scared of being alone with Kai as I believed I failed him that night by panicking. I had now fully accepted that Kai had Tuberous Sclerosis, although it would take Scott a bit longer. I told friends he had the condition, I rang the TSC association for support, I also read more about what it could mean for Kai. Yes, it was scary, but this was our reality now. Burying our heads in the sand had got me nowhere and I was ready to find out what we had in store. While reading, terrifying words jumped out from the screen: brain tumours, kidney tumours, eye and skin problems, epilepsy, ADHD, autism, delayed development, behavioural problems, Lam disease, heart problems and hydrocephalus. All were a risk to Kai but I kept reading, kept finding out. I needed to be strong for my boy.

I accepted he would probably never walk or talk, as the words he already knew were slowly disappearing. So many seizures in his short life were starting to damage him. I accepted he would probably never leave home, or drive or get married. As silly as it sounds, it's the little things that get to you - such as their first day at school or you don't get to take them, they get collected by a bus. The fact that they will never have a friend around to play or ride a bike. The little things are the things that sting the most.

Kai's birthday rolled around and we spoilt him rotten! I think we brought him most of the V Tech range of toys, although we knew he wouldn't play with them we still had hope he would acknowledge them. He got so many cards I ran out of room to put them up on display. The room was filled with presents, wrapping paper and balloons. But all Kai cared about was the chocolate cake we had brought him; he'd even tried to grab the candle out of it! We caught it all on camera his chocolatey-covered face beaming at us.

NEW BEGINNINGS

The wedding came around very quickly and, much to our surprise, it turned out to be one of the hottest days of the year that day! My house was a flurry of activity, people getting ready and the garden organised for the party afterwards. Kai was very grizzly that day as he had a throat infection and the heat wasn't helping him at all. I had my hair styled in an up-do which was curled, and had a French manicure but with a little delicate swirl over each nail and a diamond on my ring finger. I did my own make up and slipped on my dress. I loved my dress, I fell in love with it the moment I saw it and had refused to try any others on. It was white with no sleeves and had ice blue diamonds and crystals from my breast to my hips, the bottom half was ruffled and gathered at the side and then I had a long train. I had diamond sandal heels and a diamond tiara and a white veil with diamonds sewn on. I knew what Scott looked like as I was there when we choose it! It was a black three piece suit with an ice diamond coloured cravat. Kai looked gorgeous in his cream linen suit and shoes.

As I made my way down the aisle I couldn't contain my smile, I was finally going to become Vikki Hammond and share the name of my husband and son. We said our vows and both got a bit emotional. It was a lovely day with everyone we cared about in that room. We then went back to my house for a buffet and then onto the hall for the reception party. Not one thing went wrong that day, which is rare for us!

Our first dance was to Ronan Keating's song 'When You Say Nothing At All', it had a real meaning to us now after the scan with it playing. In fact, the song lyrics are so Kai that years later Scott got them tattooed up his whole arm surrounded by angels and God's hand holding Kai's… handing him back to us.

2003 was a big year for us, we had married and I had decided to go back to work as being at home all day was driving me stir crazy! My Mum offered to have Kai as she had just given up work as it was too much for her, so I went back two mornings a week. It was a bit of *me time* although I was worried sick and would call my mum on my break and rush home as soon as my shift had ended.

A new girl started, I could hear her before I saw her, laughing and joking with the other staff members. I remember my first impression of Beckie, she was straight to the point and loud I decided she wasn't really my cup of tea. However, over the next few days we got talking and she told me she used to work with disabled children and also cared for a little girl from the residential school. As she talked fondly of her memories there, I felt drawn to her and told her all about my little boy Kai, from that day onwards we started to bond but I would never have guessed how much.

As much as it killed me to admit it, my mum was getting worse, she had started to have funny little movements and her speech was slurred – a symptom of the Huntingdon's Disease she'd been diagnosed with. After talking to my dad it was decided it would be best if she didn't look after Kai anymore. So I rang work to arrange for Kai to come in with me to the nursery, he would be in the toddler group and I would be in the 2-3s but would pay full rate for him. My hours were upped to five days a week 8.30-1.00. I told my mum I had been offered more work and a package that included Kai being able to stay with me at a reduced rate, she cried and I felt terrible. But I couldn't leave him with her anymore, it just wasn't fair of either of them and it wasn't safe.

Working those five days a week, I was paired up with Beckie. We each had four children from that age range. I grew to love her, she was compassionate funny and loyal I felt like if I told her something it would stay between us. Over the months watching how she was with Kai just made me kick myself for my first impression! I never talked about Kai or what he was going through, or us, I never cried in front of people (and still find that hard to this day, I hate crying), but Beckie showed me it was OK to talk, and as dumb as it sounds, she taught me how.

Once Beckie had unlocked the feeling I had suppressed for so long it was like a weight had been lifted off me. She listened, she advised, and she kept it to herself. I talked about my mum, my nan, Kai and how all of it made me feel. She made me laugh so much I would have tears rolling down my cheeks as I held my belly begging her to stop.

Then a little boy that attended the nursery died. He was in the same set as Kai and was the same age – he'd died in a car accident. It knocked me for six, I wasn't particularly close to this little boy but it was the fact that he was young and healthy and that he had died so suddenly. It left me scared and brought a lot of things back from that night. I didn't say this, I didn't need to, Beckie just knew. It affected us all losing that little boy and his funeral was hard, seeing his little tool kit and hard hat on top of his tiny coffin began to bring my own fears to the surface, and as soon as the Bob the Builder theme tune played we all just sobbed. It was too close to home and I could feel that pain in the pit of my stomach rising.

After the funeral we went to have a drink to celebrate his life but I just sat there quietly, not talking not thinking, just numb. Beckie came over. "You go home and cuddle that boy as tight as you can." I looked at her with tears in my eyes and she nodded. "Go." That's the thing with Beckie, I don't ever have to say anything she just knows.

Kai continued to have seizures but he also continued to amaze me, I had left his dummy on the sofa one afternoon and when I walked back into the room he was standing up to reach it! My heart began to thump and I burst into happy tears. He did it, my boy was standing up! I picked up the phone and dialled Scott and a mixture of tears and shouting came out of my mouth. I just couldn't get the words out I was too excited, just then his work van pulled up, he hung up the phone and came running in the door.

"What's happened? What's the matter?" he shouted. Kai was now sitting down staring at us and listening to all of the commotion.

"Kai stood up!" I squealed.

Scott stared at me but slow relief washed over his face. "Fucking hell, woman, don't do that to me! I thought something was wrong." I put the dummy back on the sofa and we stood waiting for Kai to stand up. Bambi-like, he put one shaky little leg in front of the other and stood. Scott and I threw our arms around him and cried tears of joy. It may have taken him fourteen months but he did it.

Walking opened up a whole lot of challenges with Kai, he was so wobbly and uncoordinated and very unbalanced. He didn't see his surroundings as we did and would run into and onto things, he would run into the TV or the wall and trip over his own feet. We were constantly behind him waiting to catch him whenever he fell, and then he learnt how to climb… on sofas, tables, chairs, toys, it was actually exhausting watching him all of the time and of course he had the odd accident – you name it, he banged it. If he had a seizure he would fall to the floor but we usually had a pre-warning as he would get louder and stop running so I would sit him in my lap.

Kai was obsessed with dummies and would carry three to four around with him he would suck one or two at a time, bang one on his nose and flick the teat on the other with his fingers, he would run his dummies on the floor until they made that horrid squeaking sound. And he would hide them, we once found eighteen stashed under his bed. He would only sleep on his beloved Bob the Builder pillow case and if we ever went into hospital we would have to take that with us. He also loved food and would go out of his way to find it. He would eat off the floor or out of the bin, he was a little handful. It was around this time that Kai stopped sleeping so well and would often bang his head on his cot; I was forever going in and laying him down.

We started to get a bit of outside help as I had rung and asked for a social worker and I was very lucky to get a lovely lady called Sue. She arranged for us to attend the opportunity group every Tuesday after work until 3.00 which was a place for children like Kai to meet chat and learn. It was based in a school classroom and there were lots of activities to do such as water, sand construction and messy play. Kai hated most of these and spent the whole time spinning in circles or drinking the water from the tray and eating the PlayDough. It was the first chance I got to sit and mix with other mums going through similar issues with their children. I enjoyed these meetings as it was somewhere that Kai was just like any other child in the room.

Kai wasn't enjoying nursery, he would cry his heart out and it made it worse as he knew I was there. I considered quitting as I couldn't listen to him crying but was advised to give him a few weeks to adjust. He moved up to Joan's group and instantly those two bonded, anyone could see it they had a connection. He didn't need to do anything but Joan knew when he was hungry or thirsty or just wanted to cause mischief, and she used to help him find it! I remember once sitting with my group in the art room which had a little partition wall separating us from the other art room. All of a sudden I could hear Joan laughing and looked up to see Kai's head bobbing up and down over the wall. He was standing on the paint drying stand using it as a trampoline and Joan was behind him holding him and laughing. He got away with so much with Joan, she loved him like her own.

We then got appointments through for all different things, brain scans, eye tests and genetics. Kai's MRI came back with the news he had numerous tumours in his brain which were sparking off the seizures. He also had a SEGA which was a larger tumour that was known to grow. So we were told they would keep an eye on it. We were devastated but also prepared as tumours came with the TS. We then went for his heart scan and were told the rhabdomyomas had shrunk and two had disappeared we were over the moon!

Next came his eye test which I got myself worked up about as I have a huge eye phobia Kai's eye test came back clear we were over the moon, no tumours behind his eyes thank goodness! Next came the genetic testing –Scott and I had decided we would like to give Kai a brother or sister but wanted to know if we had the gene first. If we did I decided I didn't want anymore children. We again had to answer so many questions and fill out forms, then came the blood tests from all three of us. The results took a whole year, but waiting is all you do when you have a special needs child, as I would come to realise.

FIGHTING

Everything is waiting on phone calls, letters, results and dates, ninety per cent of the time you had to chase the hospital yourself. You are constantly battling the system for anything you need, from appointments to equipment. It is a long drawn out and exhausting process that takes its toll emotionally. Throughout Kai's life I have had numerous fights with the system from basic health care to equipment that is needed. I have had to fight for the correct appointment, and even urgent ones take months to come through. When you finally get the much needed appointment you have to deal with some consultants that are set in their ways and think they know your child better than you do. One thing I have learned through all of this is: never ever take a doctors word over something you know in your heart that is wrong.

Over the years Kai has been put on medication that was too higher dose for him, or too low. I have been told a certain health issue was simply 'nothing to worry about' on many occasions and made to feel like I am worrying and bothering them over something they believe to be of no concern. I have fallen out with many consultants as I am not one to sit back and take their word for it, I will question, pester and fight to get the right care for my son. I don't care how disliked it makes me; my boy comes first and has only me to speak up for him. If I don't, what hope does he have? I have had to fight for everything from a diagnosis to medication to results and to basic needs.

The cost of raising a child with special needs is also something I think needs to be looked at by the government. It's like ordering from a florist and mentioning it's for a wedding - the price triples. Toys for example are from £60 to over £1000, a child's adapted bike is around £600, a swing is £600. Clothing is also expensive because you can't just go to a shop and buy anything, sometimes they need all in one pyjamas (before the onesie's made a reappearance) so they can't get into their nappy, they are £30.Bibs to stop dribbling or biting clothes are around £8 each. Special non-seamed socks or special boots, the list is endless.

Special need children also have a habit of breaking things during temper or just curiosity and it's always the big things such as the TV or a brand new mobile phone. Replacing picture frames or flooring, the list goes on and on, that's not even mentioning the cost of summer clubs for a disabled child. Petrol for endless hospital visits and parking money (if they are under a certain age and don't meet the criteria for a blue badge), hospital stays, credit for your phone, congestion charges. Hospital stays are the worst, especially for a week or more it has cost us £1000s over the years. Once you have made sure the fridge is stocked and electric and gas is in credit and arranged childcare you have to try to keep the house running as well as being away from home. Then comes the time off work unpaid if you have used all your holiday and had an emergency stay booked for the hospital. Then you have to fill your car up, pay the congestion charges and park. The week itself involves money for the two of you to eat twice a day, obviously Kai would get meals from the hospital but if it wasn't suitable I would buy him something else. Then would be snacks drinks and magazines to pass the time away, emergency visits to the local shop for more wipes or pain killers or milk. Also some hospitals only allow one of you to stay so local accommodation costs are then added on.

That's before you fill the car with petrol, pay the congestion fee and get home having to restock the fridge again put more gas and electric on the meters and pay the bills. Holidays also cost more if you need accommodation with wheelchair access or a shower room etc. Food is an extra cost if, like Kai, you have to buy certain things like yellow or brown food, nothing wet only dry, certain brands of crisps etc. Even a safe surrounding for your child to sleep in is anything from £2,000-£8,000 and then there are the adaptations to your home. From 4ft stair gates that are £60 a pop, to having to chisel wires into the wall and plaster over them....

The most frustrating thing I have found that I have had to fight for is answers or results, consultants promise to call or write to you by Friday and then you don't hear from them. Everything stops at the weekend so it's just waiting for Monday morning to come, but then you phone and are put on hold, passed to the wrong department, they can't find your notes or have gone on annual leave. The worst one is the answer phone, it makes my blood boil! I have never understood hospitals not getting back to you with scan results or urgent blood tests, surely as a parent they would know how hard it is to be left not knowing? For weeks, or sometimes even months, it's pure torture not knowing.

Children with special needs are also a real cause for concern when it comes to safety. My house is bare, literally. My front room has built in shelves plastered and painted over to put a few picture frames on, but then I have placed toys in front so he can't get to them! Everything is mounted to the wall - my mirror, pictures and even the TV. As Kai used to love trying to throw that off of the stand! I have no coffee table, no ornaments, just sofas. My kitchen is bare, too; I have the obvious on the sides such as the microwave and tea essentials but the oven is chained to the wall (I'll come to that later) as is the fridge. I have a rounded table that the chairs tuck into so he can't climb. I have stair gates on the kitchen door and also the front door which are over 4ft tall, at the bottom of the stairs and at the top. I have to keep the bathroom door shut at all times as Kai likes to jump in the bath - hot or cold, fully clothed. I have extra locks on my front and back doors.

Kai's room has a safe space he sleeps in with his sensory lights and suitable toys, he has a sofa to lounge on that looks out through his patio doors. Outside has double padlocks on the gates and both big sheds are locked, we have 6ft fencing and got rid of the bark and stones for very good reason… I'll come to that later, too! We have a swing chair which he loves to sit on, and a decking area he sunbathes on. We also dug a hole to sink the trampoline into the ground so he wouldn't fall off. It was hard work and cost a lot of money but it was necessary to do for Kai's safety, which over the years he had tested us with!

We have to hide anything such as glasses, plates, bowls and anything small such as Lego or pennies. Kai likes to eat things and the kids know not to bring anything little downstairs unless they are sat at the table.

New Year came around and, as the past two years events had been awful, I was dreading it. I had begun to hate New Years and to this day have never celebrated it since. We decided to go to Scott's parents for a week as I couldn't stand to be at home on the anniversary of the day we had nearly lost Kai. So we packed the car got Kai ready and made the two hour long journey arriving there at around 7.00pm.

We literally just got through the door when Kai ran straight into the front room, I was just getting the bags from Scott when I heard a thud. I ran into the front room and saw Kai lying on the floor quite happily. And then I saw red sauce over the floor. *Where has he got that from?* I thought, thinking what I would use to clean it up. Kai rolled over to face me and I realised that it wasn't tomato ketchup, it was blood. He had cut his head wide open at the front. I picked him up and we got back in the car and drove to the local hospital. We were in there for a good few hours as Kai had to have his head glued and they had to keep an eye on him. I later learned he had found the one thing left in the room that day that he could hurt himself on - a small glass rounded table, hidden in the corner behind a chair. Kai had found it climbed on top of it and he had slipped and fell smacking his head open on the corner of the glass. Kai didn't seem fussed about what had happened; in fact, Scott and I spent the next few hours trying to stop him from spinning around in circles! We arrived back to Scott's parents around 12.30...Happy New Year...again.

Kai's seizures continued to get worse in 2004 and he was now put on Topiramate capsules that we had to open and sprinkle the contents on or into food. It went well for a few weeks but then Kai stopped eating altogether. It straight away raised alarm bells as Kai had always had a huge appetite and was very motivated by food. To get him to play with runny PlayDough (Kai hated the feeling of anything wet) Joan would put Smarties in it and he would dive across the table putting his hands in to reach them! He had loved almost anything I fed to him and would eat it and expect more! Now though, he was refusing anything he liked so I called his consultant. She advised to stick with it and see how he went. His behaviour changed and he would be very unpredictable and irritable. Those few months were a nightmare and really challenged us. He didn't want to sleep so most nights were spent up and down with him; he didn't want to eat, so food times I came to dread knowing I couldn't persuade him. His seizures were now becoming quite frightening and he was admitted into hospital on numerous occasions having to stay in overnight. His little body would shake and convulse and it would go on for minutes and then stop and then go into a different type of seizure.

After one particularly bad day Kai was having seizure after seizure I rang his consultant again. She was concerned and as it was a Friday she said she would leave an emergency prescription for me at the pharmacy in the hospital and I would have to go in and collect it. So Beckie and I put Kai into the car and drove to the hospital. As I made my way to the pharmacy I explained the consultant had left a prescription for emergency medication at the desk and I was here to collect it.

After looking around the pharmacist shook her head. "No messages left and no prescription has been left here for you."

I had had run-ins with this consultant before as I had always questioned her methods and this was the tip of the iceberg for me, I was raging. They explained they would phone her as they were sure she hadn't left the hospital yet. So I sat and listened to the conversation, she said to them she hadn't had the conversation and didn't know what they were talking about. The pharmacist relayed what was said and I stormed out enraged with Beckie following behind me.

"If Kai has a seizure that's really bad over the weekend it will be on her head!" I said to Beckie. As we talked outside the room I saw the consultant walk past and so I ran to confront her. "Why did you say you hadn't told me to come here? It's Friday afternoon, if Kai has a seizure over the weekend he has no rescue meds as you haven't prescribed him any as yet!"

She denied everything I threw at her and said she would go into the pharmacy and sort it out. So Beckie followed her discretely and heard her say she had forgot to leave one could they please write one up now. She then came back out to me all sweetness and light and explained the pharmacy had messed up and it was being sorted now. To which Beckie exploded, "I just heard you say you had forgotten! Why are you covering your back and lying?!" The doctor didn't know where to look and went red making her excuses to leave.

That wasn't my first run in with Mrs Stan and it certainly wouldn't be the last.

I insisted on an emergency appointment at Addenbrookes Hospital as Kai was getting worse, he was having a lot of seizures and his balance and coordination was extremely bad. He had so many cuts and bruises where he would run into things and fall over I lost count. We went in to see Dr James who I absolutely loved and trusted, he was the only consultant who listened and accepted what I was saying. I explained the dose he was on and the affects it was having on Kai and how his seizures had got worse over the year, not better.

He frowned. "Who put Kai on that dose?"

I looked back at him and said, "Dr Stan but I want him off them he is not the same child he is irritable moody tearful and not sleeping or eating."

Dr James looked down at his notes and replied, "He should never have been put on that dose it is way too high for him."

I was livid. I explained how I didn't trust Dr Stan and would never take her word again. We then moved onto Kai's seizures and he laid it all on the table, Kai had been given a number of drugs one of them being a very strong drug that he would have expected to work with Kai's type of seizures, we were running out of options. The only other options were the ketogenic diet, vagus nerve stimulation, or a brain operation. We talked through the three options being put to us in detail and what they would mean.

Ketogenic diet

The ketogenic diet would mean a high fat, low carbohydrate diet that forces the body to burn fats rather than carbohydrates. Carbohydrates in food are converted into glucose and travels around the body and is important in order for the brain to function. If there is little carbohydrates in the diet the liver converts the fat into acids and ketone bodies which then replace the glucose in the brain as an energy source. An elevated level of ketones in the blood leads to a reduction of seizures as it puts the body into ketosis. High fat food would replace food such as bread, pasta, fruit, sugar and more. It would mean a very strict diet where food has to be weighed measured and prepared as any mistake would set you back.

Vagus nerve stimulation

This would mean placing a surgical implant into the upper left chest and the generator is implanted into a little pouch under the clavicle. A second incision is then made in the neck so the surgeon can get to the vagus nerve. Leads are then wrapped around the vagus nerve and electrodes connected to the generator. The generator then sends electric impulses to the vagus nerve on regular intervals. Vagus nerves are nerves that run from the brain through the body, the vagus nerves send these stimulations to the brain to calm down irregular electrical activity.

Brain surgery

Depending on which part the seizure was coming from would determine the operation, but in many cases it would be a resection which would mean removing the damaged parts of the brain the seizures were coming from. It also carried the most risks.

We were told any option we choose would mean extensive testing and to go away and think about it and to be seen again in a couple of months' time.

We had a lot of decisions to make and it was so hard trying to make the right one, as much as we talked things through we were adamant we really didn't want surgery and started looking into the ketogenic diet. Around this time Kai had become horrendous with food and would no longer eat his old favourites, he would now only eat yellow or brown food. It had to be dry with no sauce, so his diet now consisted of crisps, waffles, chips, mash or roast potatoes, Yorkshire puddings, sausages, chicken nuggets and bread. That was it. No yogurts, fruit or vegetables would now pass his lips and he hated anything orange at all near his plate. It is very hard

69

feeding your child a diet of junk as you want them to have the right vitamins and nutrition and Kai was now getting very little.

By the time the appointment rolled around Kai was horrendous with food, which had also caused a few problems at work. I paid full rate for Kai to attend the nursery I was working at - which included meals, if a child was fussy or intolerant or had allergies a separate menu was made daily to accommodate this. It was fine at first; instead of his old favourites, Kai was now eating plain food so would have sausages and potato for example or sandwiches and crisps.

One day Joan came up to me upset, "The cook is refusing to give Kai a meal and would only give him bread and butter."

I looked at her in shock. "You are joking, right?" She shook her head so I marched straight over to the cook. "Why are you not providing Kai the meals I am paying for?"

She looked right at me, she was a stern woman anyway and quite blunt and to the point. I had never had a problem with her before but wasn't scared to stand my ground either. "Gemma said I wasn't to give Kai meals, he used to eat everything and is just being fussy and you are giving into him feeding him what he wants. Just make him eat what is on his plate."

I looked at her and began to shake with rage. "He isn't a fussy eater, he has lots going on you don't even know about! He is on medications that alter his taste for God's sake! I would rather him eat something than nothing!!"

70

She just shook her head and refused so I stormed down to the office but nobody was there. I went into the toilet and locked myself in, hot tears of pure rage fell down my cheeks. Why was everything a fight?!

I went home, I couldn't stay there I was so angry. When I told Scott he was livid and went to the nursery to talk to the owner, luckily she wasn't there. I went into work and was called to the office by the boss' mother, the owner of the nursery. I was so angry I was shouting rather than talking to her. But she was brilliant and agreed with me that it was ridiculous and reinstated Kai's meals - later I heard that Gemma got a good telling off.

My mum was getting steadily worse, her movement was all over the place and she would become obsessed with certain things and repeat herself. Her balance wasn't great and she would drop things and fall over. It was breaking my heart to watch her go from a strong, feisty, independent woman to someone that had no confidence and slept all day and night avoiding reality. It was heart-breaking to watch and I am ashamed to say that I started to go around to visit her less. I used to go every day, but now it was three times a week. It broke my heart hearing her voice stumbling over words and watching her twitch and try to pick things up. I tried to pretend it wasn't happening pushed it to the back of my mind and carried on but it was all to come out at some point.

A new girl started working at the nursery called Ria, she was beautiful with her long curly dark hair, dark eyes, full lips and a figure to die for. She really took to Kai and every morning she would go to the shop and stock up on peppermint chocolate and treats to share with him. He used to run straight to the baby room as soon as we entered the building and jump up and down at the door to look through the window to get her attention. She would come running to the door pick him up and swing him around and sit him on the sofa, sharing out her bag of treats with him. He would curl up on her lap, face full of chocolate, twirling her hair around his fingers and sucking it. I would walk past and they would be sharing their own private joke laughing together on the sofa. One of Kai's favourite people in the world is Ria, and she still is to this day, they have an amazing bond that I can't describe. Through Kai, Ria and I became good friends, and, like Beckie, she would later be there for me when I fell.

BALANCING

The appointment came around and we sat in the room full of doctors going over the options. Again, we were relayed the three options and talked through them in more detail. We met the lady that dealt with the ketogenic diet and she explained the foods Kai would be able to eat and the food he would have to cut out. As she went through the list of food I felt my heart sinking and looked at Scott to see he had the same feeling. Kai would never eat the food listed and every food she had mentioned he had to avoid were the only ones he could eat and his favourites. The only thing in Kai's life at this point that he fully enjoyed was food, he lived for it. He'd shut his eyes and put his fingers in his ears to block out the world and enjoy the senses he was feeling, the texture, the taste, the smell. He would now hunt for food on his own which involved him eating anything in sight - mud, stones, insects, pennies, even his own faeces...

He had taken to pulling out the contents of his nappy and smearing it on the walls in his room, he would smudge it in his fingers and run it through his hair and pop it in his mouth. The first time he did it I walked to his door and instantly could smell it, I opened the door and he was sat on the floor nappy off, poo in hand, it was everywhere. I had to bathe him, which to him was a reward in itself, whilst Scott scrubbed the floors walls and then I had to wash all the toys and bedding. He would also push over the bin and eat what he could before I got to him, at nursery he would grab off the other children's plates or out of their hands. He would eat paint, PlayDough or sand.

As I relayed this to them all in that room they were all in agreement with me, this diet for Kai would never work. Which left the VNS or the surgery. We talked through the VNS and Dr James said it didn't have a huge success rate with epilepsy as complex as Kai's, which just left the other option - surgery. I really didn't want to go down this route but what could I do? Kai's seizures were getting worse and he was getting bigger and hurting himself. Once it looked like the surgery was going to be the primary option, we were referred to Great Ormond Street hospital so they could test to see if he would be eligible before we made the final decision.

We had an appointment booked for a TS clinic in Cambridge to test Kai for autism and also to see how far he was in his development. Deep down I knew Kai had autism but found it hard to accept. Scott, however, was having none of it. "He's fine, his seizures are holding him back, once they are under control he will catch up."

I knew what he was doing as I had done it for a year of Kai's life, he was in denial. When we turned up to the appointment we were led into a room and told the whole test would take a good few hours. We sat at a little table with little chairs, next to Kai, and the lady brought out books and wooden bricks, pens and cars. That day Kai was in a very good mood so sat and explored the toys, he chewed on the bricks turning them over in his hands and banged them together and threw them. He picked up the pens and tried to eat them so we took them away; he picked up the book and again put it in his mouth. The cars were thrown across the room - to us this was good! Kai was acknowledging toys and exploring them. He was observed those next few hours and we were asked questions and she was scoring them. She then left the room and said it would take a good while for her to go through her results. So we waited, watching Kai spinning in circles, flapping his hands and blowing air out of his mouth noisily.

When she entered she sat down opposite us. "Kai's development score is coming up at 6-8 months of age," she said. I looked at Scott in shock as he stared ahead. Kai was 3 years old. "Kai also has autism and it's quite severe."

I couldn't hold it in tears streamed down my face. What next? We thanked her and left, walking back to the car in silence. We strapped Kai in his car seat and got in the front at the same time, I just stared out of my window watching the birds flying through the sky. I noticed Scott hadn't started the car so turned to him and then noticed him sobbing, head in his hands over the steering wheel.

"Scott, he will be fine, it's OK, we will get through this, he will still be our little boy."

Scott continued to sob silently, I had never seen him like this before and I started to worry. He looked up and just burst into uncontrollable sobs, his whole body shaking violently as he tried to get the words out. "My boy will never drive a car, he will never leave home or get married and he won't have his own children. Vikki, what are we going to do?"

Scott crumbled and was filled with rage for the next few weeks, he didn't want to talk about it and just shut down. I just grieved for the dreams I had for my son that he would never get the chance to fulfil. I grieved for us as a family, too. This was our first child and we had been given one diagnosis after the other without a chance to digest and accept the last. All of the things you look forward to with your first child we had been robbed of, he had lost the few words he knew now only saying Mum and bubba, every milestone he met was bitter sweet and came with a new set of problems. I was scared for us all and our future, statistics show that families with a special need child usually spilt and lead to divorce. I can see why, the stress and worry, the decisions and the heartbreak, the lack of sleep and drain on you financially - it can either make you or break you.

At this time, my nan was still battling with breast cancer and had operations to remove her breasts, it was hard seeing her in agony, wearing a wig and fragile. She was always so proud of her hair and never in the house always out at work or shopping. Oh she loved to shop and we would be out all day choosing curtains or light fittings or treating me to half a shop full of clothes. We would grab a burger and a shake. I cherished those moments, just the two of us. She never once complained of the pain and of losing her hair she just got on with it. My mum was also a cause for concern and what with everything going on I just didn't know how to cope with it all at once.

We were in talks about Kai's safety with the social services as Kai was still smashing his room up; we had to remove everything from it from curtains to toys. He would slam his head off the wall and climb on top of his wardrobe or hang from the curtains; it was no longer safe for him to be put to bed. We were told we could look into a safe space and was given an appointment to view one. When I first saw the safe space I instantly said no without even going inside. It was a huge tent a bit like the material you get in children's soft play places, even the mattress on the floor was the same material. The ceiling was strong mesh and there was a zip on the outside to do up once they were inside and a window with a zip the other side. I just saw it and thought it was a bit like a cage, I would have to zip him in at night and he wouldn't be able to get out. But he could head bang to his heart's content without the risk of injury, he couldn't climb or trash anything.

"This isn't for us," I said to the social worker, Sue.

"Why don't I leave you alone for ten minutes and let Kai explore it have a look inside and see what you think?" and she left the room.

Scott and I followed Kai into the safe space. "It's like a cage, I don't want him enclosed," I said. But Kai was banging his head off the safe space wall and laughing when he sprung back, he lay down and looked up and just seemed so content and secure. He liked it, so I had to think beyond my own feelings and think of Kai. This would be perfect, it would completely take up his whole room upstairs as they make them to measure with the door entrance at the door. The social worker came back into the room.

"He loves it," I said. And we stood watching Kai now curled up in a ball ready for a snooze. Sue explained that she would need to apply for funding as these were quite new and none were in Hertfordshire at this point. They cost £4000-£5000! So we waited.

We were given an appointment at a top hospital to see a top consultant one of the best in her field, Dr May, and so we had high hopes and set off ready to hear about the options we had already discussed with Dr James We turned up after a hectic travel to the hospital, we had used the trains as it was easier than trying to park the car… or so we thought! It was a nightmare with Kai's pram, nowhere to sit and people don't just offer so we had to stand holding the buggy tightly. Then all the lifts were out of order and as it was rush hour we had to carry the pram and Kai up and down stairs. Finally we arrived, me, Beckie and Scott, hoping for some answers from scans he had had previously and to talk through our options.

We were called into a room with around four health professionals sat around and sat down with Kai. Dr May introduced herself and we talked about our concerns how Kai's seizures were stronger and longer in length. I brought up the fact that surgery was being looked at as an option.

"Kai is not a candidate for surgery," she stated, dismissing me completely.

"Can I ask why? And can you show me his recent scan to explain why you have ruled this out?" I inquired.

She flicked through her notes not even looking at me. "Well, I haven't actually seen Kai's previous scans, they haven't been faxed over in time for this appointment."

With that I looked straight at her and said, "You are obviously wasting our time! We have come all of this way for you to rely on guess work!" I was livid; she hadn't even looked through his notes and scans to back up what she was saying. With that, I pushed Kai's buggy out of the room. "You are wasting my time," I snapped, and stormed off.

Scott and Beckie came after me and I launched into a rant of how sick I was of no one caring and taking us seriously. The doctor had no clue what living with epilepsy was doing to him or us, it was so hard to watch your child turn blue or look terrified. To injure themselves and to sit counting the seconds on the clock hoping it stopped before the five minutes were up so you didn't have to administer emergency medication rectally and phone for an ambulance. We had come all of this way and as much as we didn't want to have Kai undergo a major operation we were running out of choices. Being dismissed in such a way was enraging.

Another doctor followed me out and I explained all of this to her, I didn't like this top doctors attitude at all and I didn't see how you can write someone off without looking through their scan findings. I was also shocked that an older scan could rule out something, as with TS so much can change in such a short period of time. She asked me to go back in the room but the mood I was in I knew I couldn't come back from this rage so I refused and we left.

I got the phone call at work one morning from the results department, they had our genetic blood test results. My hands began shake as I was handed the phone. "Hi, Mrs Hammond, I am pleased to tell you both you and your husband do not have the gene."

I thanked her and hung up. We could now try for a baby! We were both in agreement this is something we wanted and needed, all of our energy and time was on Kai and as selfish as it sounds out loud we needed another reason to keep going, something else to look forward to. Kai was coming up to three and a half years old so I felt it was time. I went back to work relieved like a big weight had been lifted; we could stop tormenting ourselves with the thought that we had passed this on to Kai. As much as it is no one's fault if they pass on a faulty gene it doesn't stop the guilt and the blame you place onto yourself. Scott had convinced himself that he had given Kai TS as his granddad had epilepsy. That's the thing with guilt, you take anything you can to bash yourself with it to place the blame on yourself.

One day I was hoovering and Kai was running around in front of me when suddenly he stopped and fell to the floor. Switching off the hoover, I ran over to him to see if he was having a seizure. He was completely with it, not at all having a seizure and got straight back up again. I put the hoover away and called to Scott and explained what had just happened.

Just then his legs went and he collapsed again. We were taking no chances and took him straight to our local hospital. We explained what had happened but they seemed more interested in the fact that Kai has TS and could they bring this student in or that. I was starting to get fed up at this point as doctors and students each took it in turns to look at Kai's white patches and his shaegreen patch that was at the base of his back. A shaegreen patch is another tell-tale sign of TS, Kai's is very raised and bumpy and quite red and very noticeable. I decided to let them carry on as they had to learn somewhere, but it was irritating me at the fact that they wasn't investigating why we were there in the first place. I had come to dislike and distrust this hospital after them writing me off as an 'over-anxious mum' when Kai was a baby, and this instance was proving no different.

A doctor came in and listened to me and said it was a seizure, I stared at him waiting for him to continue. "A seizure? I know what a seizure is I have lived with them for four years! I know what all the types look like and this wasn't what it was."

The doctor excused himself and left the room. Unbeknown to him Scott had just popped to the shop to get a drink for Kai and was just walking back when he heard two doctors talking. "Mother is saying that he collapsed I have tried to explain it is a type of seizure but she isn't having it," he said to his colleague.

81

Scott marched over. "If that is my wife you are talking about in fact if she had listened to you Kai probably wouldn't be here now!"

The doctor turned red and explained they would need to scan Kai to rule out what it was but that he thought it was a seizure. So we sat and waited. Scott was fuming, I was getting angry and Kai was kicking off as he was bored. A doctor came in to see me and told me they needed to scan Kai and it would be soon. Then, an hour later he was back, they wanted to scan Kai but as he had TS they didn't know too much about it and wanted to transfer Kai to another hospital, but wanted us in overnight. I discharged him. Why would I want him to stay somewhere that didn't know enough about his condition? That comment had destroyed the little bit of faith I had had in the hospital so we took him to Cambridge. After sitting at Addenbrookes A&E they took us seriously as Kai's previous scan had shown a tumour that was capable of growing (SEGA). They told us that he was due to go back to Great Ormond Street Hospital the next few weeks and so scanned him and sent the scan over ready for our appointment there.

Great Ormond Street sent the letter for the appointments as I had asked to see someone else, appointments came thick and fast, EEG, MRI, CT scan, blood tests, to name a few. We had to stay in for a week at a time to carry out these tests which was more time off work for both of us. We had to stay in one room for a week whilst electrodes were glued onto Kai's head and then bandaged over so he couldn't pull them off. They were then tucked into a type of back pack and plugged into the wall, so he could still move around but couldn't leave the room. A camera was put in the room to record any seizures and also pick up any sounds - it was like being on Big Brother!

Any seizures he had and we noticed I was to push the button so it could be recorded and looked back on at that time. We had a pull out bed and a chair that lay down and Kai had a hospital bed. Kai was an absolute nightmare the whole week, he climbed and crawled he twisted the wires and managed to get a few off his head which had to be re-glued on. Scott was worried he would break a wire and the lady said no one had and not to worry. Well Kai did... he caused £3,000 worth of damage by twisting them and had managed to break one! We were mortified and so apologetic but she was lovely and said by the way Kai was it was no wonder! He just wouldn't sit still! So a second wire was used and we had to follow Kai around to make sure he didn't break this one!

It was a tough week being cooped up in a small room just us three and nothing much to do. Once his EEG video telemetry was complete he then had the other scans and then we were discharged.

It started gradually but I came to dread going home after work with Kai, I had isolated my friends the previous few years when I was in denial and it was hard to see anyone with how unpredictable Kai could be. I couldn't take him to anyone's home because he would climb and smash things, and also for his safety, so it was tough. I enjoyed work as it gave me a few hours to take my mind off everything, but as soon as I arrived home to an empty house it would just be me and Kai. I would have flash backs of that night, I would worry when he had a seizure and I was constantly watching him to make sure he wasn't climbing or trying to eat out of the bin. It started as dread but as the weeks went on and night time would come it would turn to pure panic. I would lay awake at night going over everything in my mind, my mum, my nan and Kai, it seemed that with everyone I loved came pain and the fear of dying. I would stare into the dark and feel my heart race and miss beats, I would shake and start to sweat and then my breathing would change - first really shallow and then really fast. I would lay there and convince myself I was going to die. This went on for a few nights and I went to the doctors, exhausted. I was diagnosed with panic attacks and given tranquilisers to help me sleep. They worked for a while but the doctor thought it would be a good idea to be referred to a counsellor, too.

I was sitting on the sofa one evening and Scott came in from work, as I sat up I bashed my breast with my arm. "They are really sore today," I said to Scott. I took a look inside my top and saw that my nipples were really dark which was unusual for me. "Scott I need you to go to the chemist for me."

He groaned and looked at me. "I've just got in the bloody door, can't it wait until tomorrow?"

I looked at him and smiled. "I need you to go and buy me a pregnancy test."

He literally ran out of the door in excitement. As I waited for him to come back I realised I was about a week late for my period but had been so preoccupied with Kai's appointments and work and my mum that I hadn't even realised. Scott came rushing back in the door and stood waiting in the doorway as I urinated on the white stick. We waited two minutes and turned it over... positive! Kai was going to have a brother or sister. We hugged each other and couldn't keep the grin from our faces all night. We told everyone straight away the excitement was too much to keep to ourselves and everyone was happy for us. I had stopped smoking and came off the tranquilisers I thought this would be something for me to focus on, something good.

Kai's result day came and we went in to discuss the results, I was a bag of nerves and couldn't stop shaking. It looked like Kai had to have another EEG and another few days stay for them to be sure but they would wait until the baby was born which wasn't too far away now but it was looking likely he would have the option of surgery. He also said Kai's SEGA had grown and they were going to keep an eye on it, he wasn't worried by this stage as they can take a while to grow to a certain size and then become problematic, sometimes they didn't continue to grow, it was a waiting game. Just hearing the fact that Kai's tumours had grown threw me into a complete and utter panic. And I knew that it would all come out at night when Kai was in bed and I had time to sit and think. I hated evenings, that anxious feeling would circle my stomach just waiting for the night time to come.

Just hearing the words 'option of surgery' played on my mind, I would torture myself with the thoughts of him dying during the operation. The decisions you make as a parent are always thought through carefully but when they are for your child's health they become an even bigger issue. I would have a million questions swimming around my head at once - what if I said yes to surgery and Kai died, or if he became brain damaged or lost part of his movement or speech? What if he couldn't cope with the pain afterwards or what if something goes wrong? What if we put him through the pain and the trauma of surgery and it doesn't work? And then the other side of me would be shouting what if you refuse and Kai has a huge seizure and dies? What if it would work and Kai would be seizure free, imagine how much better his life would be and how much he would learn. The panic would build up and rise until I couldn't breathe at all, nothing would come out and fear for the baby would set in. Scott had to take me to hospital a few times during these episodes as I just couldn't bring myself back from it. My whole body would be taken over with pure fear pulsing around my body. On a few occasions Scott had to call Ria to come over with her nebuliser as my panic attack would then set off my asthma, even at two in the morning she would drive over until Scott brought me one of my own.

Around this time I started to go online a lot, it was an escape and opened up a whole new world for me. I discovered groups where there were mums just like me; it felt good to have someone else understand what you are going through. These groups are invaluable and I have met some wonderful people over the years who I am still very close to right up to this day. They have been there through every step, not in person, but just an ear to listen and that's all you need.

The unborn baby was a huge worry to me too, every scan and every time I had to hear the heartbeat it would bring back old memories and I would wait for the scan to stop and be told the bad news. This was supposed to be something to look forward to but instead I felt the biggest blackest cloud over my head and I just couldn't get away from it. The pregnancy wasn't easy at all and I had everything from terrible heart burn to urine infection after urine infection. I ached from head to toe and would be exhausted coming home from work and then carrying on with Kai and the housework. But I had no release I had nothing in the day to look forward to, evenings were the worst time for me, so I kept going all day to take my mind off things. I cleaned everything; I still to this day clean when I am worried, it takes my mind off things. Hearing the heartbeat worried me sick hearing the thump-thump sound didn't make me happy, it just brought flash backs on. I was a walking bag of nerves and pushed Scott as far away from me as I could. This couldn't go on for much longer I couldn't cope with feeling like this.

FALLING

This is the hardest chapter I have had to write and it stirs up a lot of memories, I was in a dark, dark place and so it is pretty deep. It has taken me hours and hours to put into words how I felt when I was down, but I feel I needed to add it all as it was also a huge part of me getting back up, stronger than before.

All the signs were that this pregnancy was going well, the scans were good and we even had to have an extra detailed scan to check the babies heart and brain –we were told there was a 1% chance of our baby having TS. This in itself was a battle with me and Scott, I had told him from day one if the baby had TS I couldn't go ahead with the pregnancy. Don't get me wrong I would never ever want to change Kai, but the thought of having two children affected by the same disease was too much for me emotionally not physically. I was struggling to get by as it was. I was hiding it well from everyone, apart from night times when Scott would see me struggle to breathe and convinced my heart was going to stop beating. I would then worry about Kai, no one knows him like me he is a real mummy's boy and that in itself used to fill me with dread. I knew his cry when he was in pain or when he was hungry or thirsty or tired or needed his bum changed. I knew he would only sleep with his three dummy's and bob the builder pillow case, I also had a bond with him so strong I knew instinctively when something was wrong. Of course, Scott did too but if he couldn't work how would he support Kai? But to bring another child into the world with TS I just couldn't imagine how we would cope and would it be fair on Kai? I am in no way judging anyone that chooses to go ahead and have another child with any condition after already having one, I actually admire them, but it is a personal choice and I knew it would break me to have another child to worry about with such big complex health issues.

This pregnancy felt different to Kai's, I didn't have that nagging feeling that something was wrong.

After yet another trying week with Kai having seizure after seizure that resulted in a hospital stay, I was finding it harder and harder to keep my panic to just night times. I was avoiding my mum as much as I could, I couldn't see her like this and the guilt ebbed away at me. My dad noticed and asked why I wasn't seeing mum as much and I told him through sobs that it was killing me. It must have been harder for him as this was the woman he married and he had to watch her slowly deteriorate in front of him. My brothers were still at home and it was affecting them too, but during this dark period all I could think was about protecting myself. If I didn't see her, it wasn't happening. I could pretend that she was OK and that nothing had changed. Dad understood but told me that he didn't want me to live with guilt he knows I would feel later on, and as much as he was right I just wasn't strong enough to handle any more,so I let her down. I let them both down.

We found out we were having another boy and, so far, everything was looking normal. I didn't know how to feel about this. I was obviously over the moon that our baby was healthy and the sex didn't make any difference to us in the slightest but the guilt chipped away at me. Why was this baby alright and Kai wasn't? Was it something I did? Was it a punishment? Would I love this baby as much as I did Kai? How could I when this love was so consuming and so intense I couldn't imagine being able to equally share that love with someone else.

It was time to apply for a school for Kai; the opportunity group sat me down with the forms to help me as Kai obviously would need additional help. He was getting a lot of support at the private nursery he attended with me every day, he had funded one-to-one support. And his occupational therapist and speech therapist would visit him at the setting. Kai had coped extremely well in the mainstream nursery, although he stuck out like a sore thumb with his rocking and flapping and screeching. The children were amazing with him never leaving him out, although he wished they would. They would sit and read to him or bring their cars or building blocks over to his little chair. There was a chair at the nursery, it was a wooden Ikea chair with a blue fabric and sort of had a rocking motion, Kai loved it! I had brought him two for home as well, as he was so calm sat in the corner like a little old man! The children knew Kai loved the chair and wouldn't sit in it or if they did and Kai came onto the carpet they would move. They just sensed something was special about Kai and would ask questions like why can't he talk? But they were so accepting of him and just tried to make him feel part of the group. I think he brought out the best in them and they brought out the best in him. He would watch them sat in his chair and rock away, the kids were fascinated at how he managed to gather a steady pace with the rock, as they could never master it as much as they tried! I assumed he would go to mainstream school with extra help, but I know now I was in denial again. The opportunity group suggested Kai would need a special needs school to accommodate his needs, I agreed to look around them to humour them but I secretly had my mind set he was going to mainstream.

We arrived at the school and as soon as I walked in I saw an older child in a full-on melt down, he was head butting the wall and shouting. There were children in wheelchairs and specially adapted walking frames, children with special helmets and children that were being wheeled around with oxygen tanks. I am ashamed to say it now, but I was horrified and scared. I looked at Scott and knew he was thinking the same as me: Kai wasn't this bad, was he? And then it hit me, he may not be now but he could be, and at that moment I knew that was why they wanted Kai here. He was one day going to be the child with the helmet or in the wheelchair or having the meltdown.

I left the school in floods of tears.

We decided to go back for a second visit as we were so overwhelmed with the first we didn't take much about the school in. We were more focused on the fact that our child needed to be at a special needs school. The second time we arrived the children were sat eating their lunch in the main hall, they had a helper each and the children looked happy and calm. We were shown around and noticed they had a heated indoor swimming pool with so many toys, a little disco and light show once the lights were turned off. We were shown the outdoor area, the sensory garden, the sports field and the classrooms. We were shown the lay barn that had so many soft toys and a sensory room. I felt a sense of acceptance within me; the staff were great and the children were happy there. It wasn't the school that was wrong, it was my way of thinking. Yes, Kai was at mainstream nursery but I was there with him and it was very much free play all day. How could I expect Kai to sit in a classroom setting and be given a piece of paper and a pen, he would have no clue what to do with them. It wouldn't be fair on the children there being disrupted by him, it wouldn't be fair on the teacher having to keep stopping so she could hear the children's answers over Kai's shouting. And it wouldn't be fair on my boy. What also came with mainstream was the risk of bullying and I just couldn't put Kai through that.

I needed to change my way of thinking and get rid of that last bit of denial I had. My son had special needs and this was the perfect environment for him to be in, to learn through play in a relaxed setting with children just like him. He wouldn't stand out here, he would fit right in - my boy didn't need to change for anyone, he was perfect the way he was. Although Scott and I both shed a few tears over the loss of another dream we had, we both had to accept this is what was best for Kai.

Scott and I were at breaking point. I'd pushed him so far away from me, it must have hurt deeply, but I just couldn't handle anything else at this point in time. I used to go to bed earlier just so I could try to talk myself out of the panic and get to sleep before he did. Instead, I would lie there and feel it rising and that's the moment I thought I can't do this anymore I want to die. So I would lay there and think of ways I could kill myself so this pain would be over and I would be free from this mental torture. And then reality kicked in and I knew I couldn't leave Kai behind so I decided I wouldn't, I would take him with me. I knew I could never harm Kai and so I came up with the idea of putting us both into the car and driving into a wall at full speed. It would be quick painless and over with. Kai wouldn't have to have anymore seizures, he wouldn't have to have any operations and his little body wouldn't have to struggle to come out of a seizure. We would both be free from pain and we would both be together.

Driving to work I was thinking when would be the best time to do it, and where? It would have to be a clear stretch of road and not at a busy time as I didn't want anyone else involved in the accident. I could make it look like an accident so Scott wouldn't live with the pain of knowing I was the one that had hurt his heart so deeply. I came to a clear stretch of road one day and my hands were so tempted to let go of the steering wheel. Just let go and this would all be over... and then I felt my baby kick. It brought me back to reality I couldn't do this to Kai, or to my unborn child, I couldn't do this to Scott. I had to find the strength from somewhere to come through the other side. This was the lowest I had and have ever felt and when I look back it scares me to think how close I was to the edge.

I went to the doctors the following day and completely broke down; I sobbed uncontrollably in the chair and explained I couldn't go on feeling the way I did. It was killing me and I was worried what it was doing to my unborn baby. The doctor looked straight into my eyes. "You are on the very edge of having a nervous breakdown and have severe depression." He offered me some tablets which were safe to take during pregnancy; I took the prescription, anything to make this feeling go away. He also told me he would try to hurry up the counselling and I nodded gratefully.

I took a tablet from the pack but it just made me feel sick and dizzy, I didn't like how it made me feel, I was also worried in case it would harm the baby even though I was reassured it wouldn't. So I threw them in the bin. Counselling came at just the right time for me, I had scared myself so much and still thoughts would flash through my mind and it would take all of my will power to push them aside. Kai needed me and I had to take control of these panic attacks and get out of this deep dark place.

I was now heavily pregnant and looked forward to the weekly session, as it was a safe place to talk and to get everything I was feeling out of me, knowing it would go no further than those four walls. As much as I had Beckie and Scott I could never have told them how I was feeling at this point in time; in fact, they only learned recently how bad it had got for me. I didn't tell the counsellor about how close I had come to ending things, I was fearful she would think Kai was at risk and didn't want to put that out there. (I would tell her later on once the baby was born). I gradually started to feel a little better; just having someone to offload to that was there to just listen was all I needed. The fact that it was a stranger that wouldn't judge me was a bonus. Some days I would come skipping out of there and other days I would feel worse than before I went in, as it would exhaust me going over every emotion I had felt the last four years.

Beckie had left the nursery at this point and I was terrified, she was the only person who understood me without me having to say anything. I already felt so incredibly lonely at this point, me and Scott were just about scraping through and I knew I was adding stress to him he didn't need.

"I'm going to lose you," I said to her.

Beckie looked at me. "Just because I'm not at work doesn't mean we won't see each other, I will visit you all of the time."

I didn't believe her; after all, a lot of my friends had either gone when Kai was born through me pushing them away, or through them not knowing how to be around me and Kai. But she stuck to her word, she came over every other day and I lived for her visits. She brightened up my days and always had me laughing with her blonde comments. She also knew I never left Kai with anyone and never had a break and so she told me it was unhealthy to spend every single day with Kai, I had to let people in and trust them more. She started to take Kai out for day trips with her mum. I always missed him but felt completely at ease as she knew what to do if he had a seizure and she knew through seeing him every day at work exactly what he wanted and spoiled him rotten. He loved her and she loved him. Through Beckie I got a whole new family, her mum who we fondly call Dot is like a mum to me as is her dad, John. They are like my adoptive parents. They love Kai so much and would treat him to little presents and shower him with love. When I would go over to visit Dot with Beckie I would be completely on edge as Kai, like a mini tornado, whizzed around the house crashing into things, smearing food and climbing. As I would get up to sort him out Dot would shout at me. "Oh, no you don't! You leave my boy, he is fine. There is nothing he can do that we can't clean up!" and out would come the cake.

It was that time, my baby was starting school! He was going to be in the nursery at the school, and then the following year he would move up a class. He would stay there until he reached the age of eighteen so he wouldn't need to be disrupted or uprooted. As I started to change his nappy and dress him in his smart, little uniform, the tears escaped my eyes. My little boy was starting school and he had no idea, not a clue where he was going.

A school minibus would collect him and return him every day as it was a trek from my house to his school; this was provided through the council for disabled children. I wouldn't be there to kiss his little blond head and straighten his coat and wave at the school classroom door. I wouldn't be there to comfort him and see what he was up to everyday. He was out of my sight five days a week; after being with him 24/7 I would find this so hard. As I kissed him and handed his bag over, I shut the door and tried to busy myself getting ready for work, and couldn't wait for him to return home so I could smother him in kisses!

It was weird walking into the nursery and seeing the little blue chair empty, not seeing his little head pop over the wall as I sat painting with the children. Kai settled in after a few weeks, he was a bit tearful (my fault as I had smothered him so much the last few years he was always by my side). But he seemed to like it and gradually used to stand by the stair gate waiting for his bus to arrive.

Finally the day to go on my maternity leave arrived and as I walked into the nursery all the children and staff were standing in the main area holding cards and presents. I was overwhelmed as they handed me vouchers and baby clothes and a bouncy chair and even a few bits for myself. I was happy to be leaving as I was very big and uncomfortable at this stage and getting very tired. Also, it didn't seem the same without Kai there, but I would miss my friends and of course the children. I was worried about being at home on my own so much as it gave me time to think and that had given me every reason to hate being not busy! I didn't think it would be for long, I would come back with the baby when he was nearly one. But things didn't go to plan.

Two weeks before my due date and I was fed up, completely fed up, I was heavy achy and ready to meet our baby. I was due on the 19th January, two days before Kai's birthday. I had read that sex brings on labour and so I said to Scott let's give it a go. Minutes later I had my first contraction, then my 'show'. I rang Beckie so she could come and sit with Kai but I felt terrible as it was 11.30 at night. I then called the midwife who advised me to have a bath and wait to see what happened. After my bath I was standing in the kitchen in a towel talking to Scott when my waters broke, we both looked at each other. This was it, we were going to meet our boy.

We arrived at the hospital and my contractions, by this point, had stopped and so I was offered to wait or to be induced. As inpatient as we are, we decided to be induced, which I regretted instantly as the pain came on thick and fast. I was quite emotional during the labour as I was still terrified something would be wrong with our baby. After six hours of pure pain I pushed our baby into the world at 6.25am on the 4th January 2006. He had jet black hair that stood on end, big brown eyes and a little squished nose. Scott was instantly in floods of tears as they passed him to me.

As I looked down at this beautiful baby boy, we had decided to name Bailey, I felt that usual panic feeling rising from the pit of my stomach.

"What's wrong?" Scott asked.

I carried on looking at my baby, waiting to feel the hit of pure love but it wasn't there and I was terrified. I felt empty and felt nothing. "I just need a drink, please can you go and buy some," I asked, trying to get Scott to leave the room, and so off he went. I continued looking at this little boy, his face all screwed up and still I just felt pure panic, and then he cried. He let out a little squeaky hungry cry, his little fists were screwed up and he was moving his mouth into me to get his fill of milk. I was handed a bottle and as I fed him I finally felt it – pure, raw, emotional love came crashing down on me. I felt relief wash over me as we sat together in that room, this little boy needed me as much as I needed him and I wasn't going to let him down.

We stayed in hospital for a few days as I had strep B in this pregnancy, so antibiotics were administered through a drip during labour. Strep B is a bacterium found in quite a few people and is harmless, but during labour if it is passed to the baby it can be life threatening and lead to meningitis. Bailey was a good weight of 8Ib 2ozs, not bad for two weeks early! A nurse entered the room to move us upstairs and checked on Bailey.

"He's making funny little sounds, I need to go and get him checked as it could be an infection," she said.

My heart sank. Not again. Why couldn't I just have a baby to hold with no worry? I sat waiting for ages twisting myself up, my tummy in knots, then she finally brought him back into the room.

"He is fine, he is just a naturally noisy baby!" And he was! He used to grunt and groan himself to sleep, he couldn't sleep unless he was making a noise, but that's Bailey he never shuts up to this day! I still couldn't relax even after Bailey had all of his checks, and so the midwife called the paediatrician down again to see me. He was a lovely man and went out of his way to help put my mind at ease.

"Look, we will both check together for white patches," he offered, and together we took each item of clothing off as we scanned the whole of his body from head to toe. But I still thought it was too good to be true, after all, Kai was sent home and look what happened. We were discharged and I couldn't wait to take him home to see Kai, I was worried Kai would think he was being pushed out, or he would hate the noise. But Kai just didn't acknowledge him at all. He would if I handed him and sat with them both on my lap. but otherwise he would just ignore this child that had invaded our home. He gave him the odd kiss on the head but that was as much attention as Bailey would get… until he was walking!

It was so strange having a child that didn't have seizures, a child that met each milestone with ease. I couldn't get used to it and would wind myself up thinking we were missing something. He was a happy, chunky baby who was fascinated with Kai and his little ways, he laughed at his whizzing and spinning and imitated his flapping and rocking. But didn't get anything back in return which was heartbreaking. I was still having the odd panic attack, but having a new baby had stopped the night time obsessing as my body was ready for sleep as soon as my head hit the pillow, and so I had a few months of pain free mindless sleep. It wasn't to last.

"Kai's seizures are coming from his left temporal lobe and the area is suitable to operate on, we are not certain of how much, if any, this would reduce the seizures, but Kai is a candidate for surgery,"Dr Hank said. It was sort of what we wanted to hear, we had an option to fall back on if things got really bad, and then came the bombshell. "Kai also has a giant cell astrocytoma (SEGA) as you know from a previous scan, but it has grown. We wouldn't usually expect to see it grow so fast in a young age."

I just stared at Scott opened mouthed. "What does this mean?" I didn't want to ask the question as I already knew what was coming.

"Well, as I said surgery for epilepsy is an option for you to consider, but I'm afraid if left at the rate this SEGA is growing it would mean Kai could die." Those were the words that I had been dreading hearing out loud, the words I had tried to push to the back of my mind and those were the words that would cause me to fall.

Dr Hank was a lovely man and very sympathetic in the way he spoke, I liked the way he talked to Kai as well instead of ignoring him. I could feel hot tears in my eyes but kept swallowing to hold them back. I had no option, Kai had to have this surgery or he would eventually die, we were told it was urgent and would need to be done within the next eight weeks. If we were to go ahead with the epilepsy surgery, that would then be done eight weeks prior to the first. I explained to Dr Hank about the head banging and the erratic behaviour and the collapsing episodes. Kai had started to slap his head as if in pain and was violently head banging off the walls. He was

101

starting to climb more and smash things and cry for no reason. And of course he had collapsed but it had been brushed off. The doctor explained we had to keep an eye on Kai and if any similar symptoms were to happen then we would have to bring him straight into our local hospital. I knew there was a reason Kai was falling, and I was angry, again, that I hadn't been listened to. You are supposed to trust your local hospital but they had let us down a few times and it was hard to have any more faith in them. It was all too much and I rang Beckie, sobbing that the decision was taken from us; Kai *had* to have brain surgery no matter what. We were shocked the SEGA had grown so much in such a short period of time and the harsh reality was if we hadn't of had those scans we wouldn't have known until the flowing year, and by then it would have been too late.

Those next few months of waiting were hell. The panic attacks returned and were now worse than ever. Even if I had managed to get to sleep I would be jolted awake by a sense of pure fear as my heart raced. I was no longer at peace even in my sleep.

I stopped eating, it's something I do when I am very stressed, I lose all of my appetite completely. Trying to force a mouthful of food into my mouth just makes me feel physically sick. Even if I did manage to get food in it would stick in my throat, I was so tense my body was telling me this was too much to handle. I started smoking again - much to Scott's disappointment -it was the only thing that gave me a sense of release five minutes of blowing out my worries. It helped a little, I was a little less tense when I smoked, but I also felt incredibly guilty as I smoked outside when I needed one, as I had a baby nine-months-old and here I was outside stinking of smoke. Scott and I started to come a little closer together again, we started to bond through fear. We were too scared to voice our fears out loud to each other, so I voiced them to my counsellor. What if Kai was further set back by this op? Or he didn't pull through. I had a release every week, a place to get it all out, but Scott didn't. He kept it all in until the day came for us to hand over our son.

I knew we had no choice, he had to have this operation and in a way it was a sense of relief as the choice was taken out of our hands. We didn't have to agonise if this operation was right or wrong or if it would benefit Kai. We didn't have to weigh up the pros or the cons, if he didn't have this operation he would die. I already had experienced a few minutes of Kai not here when he had stopped breathing and the pain I felt in those moments I would never ever forget. It was a deep physical pain and as desperation set in I knew and know now that could never carry on my life without Kai in it. I couldn't function a day without my boy, we are linked in such a deep way, more than a mum and son bond, it went deeper. I know Kai in such a way that I know when something is wrong and I know exactly when I should be worried. Although this brain operation was going to be tough on all of us, Kai more than anyone, I didn't have any bad feelings, just 'what ifs'. We had made a decision about the epilepsy operation after many hours talking, disagreeing, and then trying to talk each other out of the decision we had made. We both agreed we had to try this, we had to give Kai a chance at a seizure free childhood, drugs were not working, we had no other options, it was time to stop being selfish Kai needed this chance. But why did I have a terrible feeling that this operation wouldn't be plain sailing? We also knew that Kai having such a major operation would mean his safety had to be looked at. His room wouldn't be safe for him after as I was scared he would head bang off the walls. So my amazing social worker pushed as hard as she could to get the safe space delivered and in place ready for Kai's return from the hospital.

Kai's operation date was 2nd November and we had to be in the day before, so we threw a little firework display in the garden as we knew Kai would miss out on the bright lights and hotdogs. We had a little moment in the garden, me, Scott and Beckie, as we stood watching the colours burst into sprays of light as they hit the dark sky.

The day came for the operation, Beckie was having Bailey and for this I will be forever grateful as she knew him like her own. We arrived at the hospital early so Kai could have his pre-op tests. We were then given the hotel across the road from the hospital for the night as it is run through a charity, and would be a pain to go home and come back early as Kai was first on the list for the following morning. The day dragged by slowly, we explored the local town walking around looking at shops but our hearts weren't in it. The night was even longer, we were tossing and turning as Kai fell into an exhausted sleep.

Morning came and Kai wasn't allowed to eat or drink so we packed up our things and made our way across the road, the short walk was quite hard as we wheeled Kai in his pram, flapping his little hands away and looking at the sky. I felt guilty as he had no idea what was about to happen to him and it felt like betrayal in a way. We made it back to the ward and went over the consent forms. My hands shook as I signed my name on that piece of paper.

"Kai is first on the list," the nurse said, handing us a gown to put on Kai.

We sat looking at the clock and I turned to Scott. "I can't do this, can we just pick him up and run?" I said, eyes brimming with tears.

I knew Scott was feeling the same way but he looked straight at me, "And then what? We have to do this we have no other option."

I knew he was right but instinct just wants you to protect your child. My dad arrived at the hospital to support us; he had left my mum at home. He sat looking at Kai and his eyes were twinkling with tears. The nurse entered the room, it was time. We walked slowly down the corridor and into the room, we were both allowed in to see him put to sleep, my dad would wait outside. As Kai was sat in the chair in Scott's lap a mask was placed over his face, I watched as my energetic little boy's hands started to slow down, the motion of his flapping eyes flicked back as his little body fought to stay awake and get the mask off. Finally, he fell to sleep. We both kissed him on the head and told him how much we loved him, and walked out hand in hand. The three of us stood in the corridor and just cried out of fear for our little man that made every day worth getting up for.

The nurse took our numbers and told us to go for a walk as it would be a good four hours until the operation would be completed. Those four hours were the worst of my life. We had our phones glued to our hands. We didn't know what to do for the best so we sat in the ward room, but it drove me crazy seeing Kai's Bob the Builder pillow case and his Tommie Tippee cup. And so we walked the streets of London, not anywhere in particular we just walked to pass the minutes by. I was exhausted but kept walking; it was freezing cold and icy so we sat in a cafe. We felt so guilty sitting there drinking whilst Kai was on an operating table, but it was somewhere out of the cold. We started to make our way back to the hospital, three hours had already passed and I was hoping we would get a call any time now, so we upped our pace and went back to the ward. We sat for another hour and as it passed I felt my stomach churn with fear and aching to see my boy again. Finally after almost five hours in we were called down to recovery, it was only mum and dad allowed in so we said goodbye to my dad as he had to get back to my mum.

Kai was lying in a bed in the corner, tubes and wires were in and out of him, his little head was bandaged and he was fast asleep. He had a drain attached from a tube from his head to drain away fluids and he was wired up to monitors. He looked so vulnerable and so little lying there in that bed as me and Scott took it in turns to kiss his little hands.

We were to stay there until they had run observations over the next hour or so, and then he would be moved onto the ward. They had to move his feet and arms to check for signs he was waking. We were worried as it had been explained to us that there was a risk Kai could lose feeling down one side. So after a few attempts he moved his right arm and both legs but not his left arm. We were worried this was everything we had feared and the nurse also expressed concern. After an hour Kai moved his left arm and we both let out a big sigh of relief. He had got a dead arm from lying slightly on his side.

It was time to be wheeled up to the ward and we followed behind the porter with the trolley bed, as we walked we could see people stepping aside with sympathy in their eyes the same way I used to when I saw a child on a trolley after an operation. The hospital staff were great and allowed Scott to stay the week as well as me, they weren't busy and so they bent the rules which I was immensely grateful for as I really didn't want to be alone.

Kai woke from his sleep and was dosed up on morphine so was quite comfortable, although his throat was sore from where the tube was inserted during surgery. He had a few sips of drink - and later ate lots of chips! I rang everyone to tell them the good news.

My nan was so pleased and burst into laughter shouting to everyone at her house. "Kai is in bed eating chips, can you believe it?"

My boy never failed to amaze us. He didn't cry or complain at all and was more worried that he had something on his head (he hated hats!) and was trying to get it off by slyly itching and then pulling at the bandage. The surgeon came around and explained that the operation was a success and he had removed all of the SEGA. I could have kissed him at that point

107

and it took all of my energy not to throw myself at him for a great big hug! Scott and I were buzzing, Kai looked well and the operation had been a success. We got the best night's sleep that night, a peaceful, stress-free sleep.

The next day Kai was sitting up and demanding to be fed, he had a few visitors who all brought his favourites like Wotsits, Quavers and milky buttons. Beckie came in with Bailey and I hugged my boy tightly. I had missed him so much and drank in his baby smell. As soon as Beckie saw Kai she burst into happy and relieved sobs and cuddled into him. Kai didn't acknowledge Bailey, he so wasn't a baby person at all, but was happy to see his Beckie. The next few days Kai was up walking and seemed happy and pain free, we were allowed home on day five and they said it was one of the quickest recoveries. We were shown what symptoms to watch out for in case of infection and also told how to care for his head, no swimming, no bouncing and no physical activities. Which was easier said than done, there is no stopping Kai!

We arrived home with big smiles on our faces and made up a bed for Kai to sleep on downstairs during the day so we could keep an eye on him. He napped a lot which was good as it meant he was still and not running around. It was lovely to have our family back together. And also I couldn't wait to see Kai's safe space, we walked up the stairs and opened his door. It was perfect, completely safe with no risk of him climbing, escaping and he could bounce his head without the risk of injury. Later that night we took Kai in his new room and he loved it, it would really change our life that little blue tent.

Over the next few days the swelling was really bad, his eyes were like slits and his head was puffy and felt like jelly to touch. I rang the ward who assured me it was normal, and so I felt at ease. We gave Kai pain relief every four hours and he coped just fine. The hardest thing for Kai was the lack of school, he really missed it and waited by the gate for the bus every day, but of course Kai wouldn't be going back to school for a few months yet as we still had the next operation to come.

The next few weeks the panic attacks started to come back, again I tried to hide them from Scott and went to bed before him. I was now obsessing over the next operation, I just had a bad feeling about this one that I couldn't shake off. I started to dread waking up in the morning as each day was a step closer to the operation. I started smoking a lot and again my appetite decreased, I cleaned more and dreaded the night times and again just wanted to go to sleep and not wake up. I was a walking bag of nerves and this depression had such a hold of me which I hated. It felt like I had nothing to look forward to and everything ahead of us was waiting or not knowing or going through things like this. I resented people that could look to the future, as I couldn't and still can't think ahead by more than a month, it scares me too much.

Nothing was certain with a disabled child, there was always a new health scare or a new diagnosis, and of course there was my mum. I hardly saw her now and it was easy as I was concentrating on Kai, but as my counsellor had said you can't deny what is in front of you. It was a way of protecting myself from the reality of the situation, and also my body's way of saying it couldn't take on any more.

This was the lowest point for me and I used to daydream of ways I could end things, fantasising about how free I would be. But reality would pull me back, I couldn't leave my boys. I wasn't living, I was existing. I didn't laugh anymore or enjoy anything, instead I focused on the operation. I was ashamed that these feelings had resurfaced, after all, it was Kai that was going through all of this not me, but I was terrified something would go wrong and I was right.

The day came for the operation, it was now January and Christmas had passed with a cloud hanging over us all. Again Beckie would have Bailey for us, he was now one and full of little words and exploring the world. I hated the thought of leaving him behind, especially so soon after the last stay away from home, but we had to give this a try as Kai had to have a chance at a life with reduced or no seizures.

This time they couldn't allow us both to stay as it was busier and there was no room, I felt sick at the thought of being alone after what was about to happen. We couldn't afford a hotel and the charity hotel was full, we couldn't afford the travelling to and from the hospital everyday either so Scott had no choice. He didn't want to leave Kai or me and so he said he would sleep in the car, I was horrified it was January and bitterly cold outside but he said there was no way he was leaving us. He would stay all day and then leave when he was asked to and then come straight back first thing in the morning. He would do all of that for us, which is exactly why I loved this man so much, as much as I felt alone those few months Scott was always there by my side going through the same as me.

Kai was taken down to theatre and I decided I couldn't go in this time as it killed me to have to hand him over and watch him struggle. Scott took him in as I kissed my boy goodbye and hugged him tightly. "I love you so much, and mummy will be here when you wake up," I said. Kai was oblivious and flapped and twisted his hands in front of his face.

When Scott returned we cuddled and this time it was his turn to fall as he sobbed in my arms. The same routine as last time, wandering, looking at our phones and hanging around the ward waiting to be called to see our boy. This operation took four hours and every minute dragged as we tortured ourselves with the wondering - had we made the right decision? Finally, we were called into recovery to see him. As before, he had wires and drains in and out of him, he responded to the observations and the trying to wake him up. And we were taken upstairs to the ward. From the minute we got back to the ward Kai wasn't happy, he wasn't in any pain but was restless and his throat was much sorer for him to drink and eat, although he still did. The surgeon came around and explained he had removed the tubers that were causing the seizures and he had to remove a part of his brain too. He was happy with the surgery and we would just have to wait to see if it had worked. The next day Kai's face came up in a huge rash, as did his chest, it was hot to touch and was very angry looking and itchy. It turned out Kai had an allergy to Elastoplast and where the tube had been taped down was where he was in discomfort. Already I started flapping, I knew something about this operation wouldn't be as plain sailing and was terrified something else would happen, and I was right.

Scott had been travelling back and forth to the hospital as he couldn't stay so this stressed me too. Hospitals are very lonely, boring places, especially when you were as anxious as I felt. Kai was up and walking and, although itchy, was all right. We were told we would probably be allowed home on day five if all was well.

The next night after the surgery I was fast asleep on the pull out bed diagonal to Kai's hospital bed when I woke up with a start. I could hear Kai awake so sat up to look at what he was doing in the dark, I turned on the lamp and my heart stopped. Kai was standing up in his bed a few feet off the floor. If anyone has stayed in a hospital you will know the beds are quite high even when lowered on the lowest setting. I had voiced my concern about the height of the bed before but Kai was too big for a cot and this was the only other option. He stood flapping in the dark as I quietly tried to get up without making a sudden movement to startle him. Before I could reach him he tripped on a wire and went straight over the safety bed guard and landed on the hard tiled floor, smacking the back of his head.

I screamed as loud as I could and pressed the alarm, I ran over and Kai was crying holding his head. I felt terrible I could see exactly what was going to happen but couldn't stop it, I felt like the world's most useless mum at that point in time. The nurses, hearing my screams and seeing the alarm, came running in. We got Kai up and I was crying with panic, he had only just had surgery hours before and now he had smashed the back of his head on the floor. The nurses had to do lots of observations on him and called the doctors to see what they should do. They were worried Kai could now get a blood clot and so he had to have a scan, I was cursing myself, I knew it, I knew something was going to happen with this operation, why did I choose to put him through this? I rang Scott in a state and he made his way back to the hospital, he calmed me down and cuddled Kai tight. This boy would one day be the death of us!! The scan came back normal but we had to stay in an extra three days to keep an eye on him, Kai wasn't bothered, he was up and ready to spin hours after...

Those next few days dragged but I was happy to stay in longer as I was worried about the accident, finally on day eight we were allowed home. Kai was happy to be home and was recovering well, he was sleeping, eating and happy and so I thought I could relax now he was out of the woods.

However, over the next few days Kai started screaming in pure agony, he was rolling around on the floor and nothing I did would console him. I rushed him to the hospital where they ran tests, it turned out he was very badly constipated after all of the anaesthetic he had had the last few months. We were prescribed some medicine to loosen him up and sent home, this went on for weeks. He would sob in pain and I would cry with him blaming myself for the pain he was in. I was falling back into a deep depression watching Kai suffer so much; constipation, as simple as it sounds, is pure agony and cramps are horrid. He wasn't sleeping and neither was I.

The next few days his swelling came out, all his eyes were puffed up and his head boggy and soft again. I was washing his hair in the bath when I noticed two lumps behind his ears they felt like bone, they were rock solid and huge. I pulled his ears back and could see them, again I rushed him to hospital. Kai's wounds had become infected and the lumps were glands that had raised behind his ears. My poor baby, what next? I was so scared of losing Kai that I tried to emotionally distance myself, I could do it with my mum. I went through the motions of caring for him, but tried not to think too deeply, and tried to talk myself into what life without Kai would mean. As horrible as this sounds, I feel I need to include this as it is how I honestly felt at the time, I felt I was going to lose Kai and so was mentally preparing myself for when this would happen.

It all came to a head one night when I had the biggest panic attack ever and ended up in hospital. I just couldn't breathe at all and was rushed in and put on a machine, after I had calmed myself down enough to be discharged I declared that I was no longer going to be weak, I was no longer going to feel like this, I was tired, exhausted and mentally drained. My body was screaming at me to eat, sleep and stop thinking. I went back to the doctor who diagnosed severe depression and I was referred back to the counsellor. Keeping this locked inside was poisoning me, my family, and my relationship with Kai. I had to stop being selfish, stop wondering what if and find some strength from somewhere, and I was determined.

STRENGTH

After the stages of grief comes strength. When you have been through denial, loss and heartache you have to find strength to carry on. I often get told how strong I am, but those that know me well know I am not. I am good at putting on a smile, good at hiding my emotions and good at pretending everything is OK. I am a worrier, I worry about the future, I worry how Kai is feeling, and I worry if everything is affecting the children. I just worry in silence. A big reason why I became so unwell, which caused me to fall, is because I am very guarded, I don't talk much about my feelings, hence why this book took so long to write… it's like therapy.

I no longer cry and if I do it is in private, I hate crying, I see it as a weakness in me. Crying takes me back to all of those years when I was unwell and in that very dark place, and I never ever want to go back there. I am good at shutting things out, instead of talking I write letters to myself about my mum, Kai, my nan and whatever else that is on my mind. I am not good at expressing how I feel, so if Beckie thinks I'm worrying I send her the letter to read, as it's easier than talking, then she understands. It frustrates Scott a lot as sometimes he just wishes I would break down and say what I am feeling, but it is rare that I do that these days.

Beckie and I took the kids to Pizza Hut for lunch one day, I had forgot to bring Kai's Tommie Tippee cup and he, at this point, wasn't good with a cup. Beckie offered Kai a Fruit Shoot which in the past had failed as he couldn't work out how to suck it. He took it from her hand and sucked it straight away! Just then the lady came over to take our order but Beckie and I couldn't speak as we were in tears of joy!

"Sorry for the state of us but he has just drank a Fruit Shoot for the first time," Beckie said, the woman looked at us as if we were mad as we snapped away pictures and rang everyone to tell them! It is the little things...

I had started to take Bailey to all the things I could never do with Kai as he was so unstable and didn't like noise or change or was in hospital. We went to swimming groups and toddler groups. It was like I was living two different lives, this was the life that was 'normal' and then I had the other life which not many can relate to. It felt very weird to feel normal after so many years being isolated and I looked forward to my weekly groups. I met some very special friends through these, Sarah being one of them. She has always been very loyal to me, very honest and very real. She has been a shoulder to cry on and someone to kick me up the arse and tell me I'm better than the moping crap! She still is a good friend to this day.

People often ask me: how do you do it? And I reply, what choice do I have? If I didn't carry on who would care for my children? You just have to, it's the cards you are dealt and you learn to adjust and make the best of it. People also often say I couldn't do what you do, but they could. If faced with the fact that your child would be born or become disabled you just *do*. You have no choice. Having a disabled child doesn't automatically make me a great mum, it just makes me a mum, it's what we do. Everyone, when faced with problems, learns how to deal with it and gains strength though the process. My nan for instance, I never once heard her moan or complain. Neither did my mum, they had been given these horrendous diseases but they had a choice they could give up or fight. And, in their own ways, they chose to fight. Those are the strong ones to me, not me; I'm just an ordinary mum to an extraordinary boy.

People's attitude's against the disabled is something that makes my blood boil, there are many situations you are faced with as a mum, some are infuriating and other situations are heart-breaking. I know all parents who have a disabled child have experienced some of these and to help you understand I'll explain. A few I have encountered have added to my strength to keep going for Kai and to keep fighting, I am his voice and without it what does he have? I've felt peoples' stares and nudging when I wheel Kai past them, I can see and hear you, it hurts.

I can hear your whispering and comments, it hurts. I can see the sympathy looks - and this is the worst insult to both me and to Kai. We don't need sympathy, I am lucky to have such a clever, courageous child and I wouldn't change him for the world. I pity you for never experiencing the joy a child like Kai can bring to your lives, making the simplest of things seem like a miracle. I have had children laughing and staring and, to me, that is sad. It just shows that their parents haven't educated them on how different each and everyone in the world is. As I tell my children, we are all different – race, gender, appearance and abilities – we shouldn't judge on any of these things. I have had a grown man ask me if my child was a spastic, I have had people pat my arm and say 'poor boy'. I have had a woman physically repulsed at the fact that Kai dare go up and touch her. I have had unwanted advice from complete strangers at the fact that Kai had a dummy at the age of four. But, what I do like is people approaching me and asking questions, this does not offend me in the slightest. I would rather be asked why does your son have those scars on his head? Why is he in a wheelchair? Why is he making that noise? Than be stared and gawped at. I love children, they just come right out with whatever is on their minds, and they ask the question the parents are too afraid to. The parents usually nudge or try to shut the child up, but I honestly do not mind. It is teaching them that it is OK to ask why something or somebody is so different. In fact, I wish more adults had this approach.

A few questions that can sting but I still answer, and I know some people are dying to ask are the following: "He looks so normal, you would never know anything was wrong with him." Yes, Kai physically looks 'normal' and sometimes that is harder as people are less accepting. If someone looks alright then they must be, right? I have often wondered how peoples' opinions would be if Kai's appearance was different. Another one is: "Is it genetic?" I can sometimes take this the wrong way, it is sort of implying that it is somehow my fault even though if it was genetic it still wouldn't be my fault, but it is how it makes you think. Another one is: "Will he grow out of it?" Simple answer is no, of course not, if only it were that simple. The next is: "Why did you carry on having more children?" Simple answer, why not? We had the genetic testing and decided to take the 1% chance as we wanted a family like any other couple do. These are the only questions that can hurt a little, but I understand peoples' curiosity and so I don't take it personally.

Through these situations it adds to your strength and makes you more determined than ever to carry on. On a bad day, if I'm fed up of the stares, I do sometimes shout at them to embarrass them! I've had the older generation shout at me when I pull up with Kai in a disabled space, "This is a disabled space." They shout at me in anger. I just smile and shout back, "Well lucky me, I have a disabled child and a wheelchair, does that count?" usually shuts them up. Scott is worse in situations, it really hurts him when someone stares and he is hot headed so they usually get a mouthful off him whilst I cringe and hang behind!

After Kai recovered from his operation I started to feel the black cloud lift, I could see the sun again and felt happy at each new day instead of dread. Kai had a small seizure a few days after the operation but we were told this was normal and not to go by this, time would tell. Kai was off school for a good few months, the operations had taken its toll and he was a little unsteady - still suffering from constipation - but otherwise seemed to get better as the days went on.

It was hard those few months as I was house bound with him, I couldn't risk the park and couldn't take him swimming and so we had very little to do. Kai didn't like much else, he wouldn't sit still at a cinema and he didn't like those indoor ball places. It was very hard those months as each day felt the same, the same routine, the same staying in and with the cold weather the garden was out of bounds. Scott was working so I longed for Beckie's visits just adult conversation and a different face to look at. She was amazing over those months helping to bath him and dress him and give him medicine. So, when I was offered respite through the social services, I refused. It just wasn't for me. I wanted my boy at home with me, not somewhere else, and whilst I was physically able it would stay that way. As much hard work as Kai can be I just couldn't send him to respite and I was offered direct payments instead. This is where you employ someone to come in for a set amount of hours each week and the money gets put into an account, I then pay their tax using this money and pay their wages. Again I refused, I wouldn't feel comfortable with a stranger in my house and around

Kai, I have trust issues so couldn't see this working. Until they mentioned it can be someone I knew, and it was obvious to me then, who cared for and treated my kids like their own? Who could I trust more than anyone? Beckie.

I sat her down and told her about the offer, I didn't want her to feel that she had to take on more as she was already working in the day. But she jumped at the chance, it was good for all of us, Beckie was virtually here every day anyway unpaid and always insisting on helping. Kai loved her, so did Bailey and both Scott and I loved her like a sister. To this day she still gets paid to come in three evenings a week for a couple of hours and a Saturday where we usually take the kids out. Scott trusted her so much he gave her her own door key to come and go when she needed. He says she's like the sister he never had.

We went on a little holiday to Wales through the TS association. I got a phone call asking if we would like to go as they knew what had been going on recently. We jumped at the chance and off we went. It was a beautiful group of little cottages that was owned by a lady, she would rent out the two guest cottages to disabled families. It turned out another family was there with a ten year old with TS and she asked if we would like to meet them. It was a tough decision as it was like we were going to get a glimpse of what life could be like in a few years' time.

The family were lovely and they had two children. The little boy, Jake had severe seizures and wasn't a candidate for surgery, drugs were barely helping. He was able to say a few words like Kai, but not much and needed twenty four hour care, he was in a wheelchair but could walk short distances. It hit me hard, one thing I really did fear was the thought of a wheelchair and it's hard to explain why. Although it makes sense in my head it doesn't out loud. It's like a label that says 'I'm disabled' and although I knew Kai was, it was scary to think that he could need us that much and not use his legs like we did. Scott and I both said we didn't think Kai would ever need a wheelchair, he enjoyed running and walking and we used the pram as more of a safety thing. They explained that Jake was just like Kai, he used to run and walk but, as the years went by, he got more tired and unbalanced. It really shook me, he was also fed through a tube and again they explained that he, like Kai, used to love his food but had stopped eating a couple of years before. I was crushed, that's the thing with TS you never ever know what is around the corner.

We had a lovely time walking through the town and exploring the beach, one day walking along the beach Kai started to up his pace. Scott was showing Bailey the sea so I ran after him, but he was too fast and then I saw what he had spotted and I ran faster. By the time I got to him Kai had sat himself on a ladies lap and was eating a sausage off their barbeque. I was so embarrassed and couldn't apologise enough, the poor shocked lady was fine and was trying to hide her giggles.

Another day we walked through a restaurant and I was holding Kai by the back of his t-shirt (he hated holding hands then) when all of a sudden he threw his arms out and grabbed a steak right off a man's plate. I just wanted the ground to swallow me up there and then and went bright red. Scott was full of apologies but the guy was fine and said not to worry. I wanted to leave there and then but Scott wanted food and by the looks of it so did Kai! So I sat there hiding my face.

Kai was getting bigger now and his pram was no longer practical as his feet were on the floor, so we got referred to the wheelchair services and got given a Maclaren major pram, it's exactly like a pushchair but double the size and has a foot tray. It really helped as Kai couldn't walk far and when he did he was unpredictable and would dart off from my grip or have a seizure or trip over something. I didn't mind the pram although it looked different it did the job perfectly, but when I took Kai out in it I would get stares as if I was a lazy mum who just wanted the convenience of my child wheeled about rather than deal with him. I'd hear tuts of disapproval and see nudges - until Kai rocked, flapped or groaned and then the penny would drop and they would turn away. As I said, as Kai didn't look disabled it was harder for people to understand anything could be wrong.

Kai's safety was becoming a huge issue for us at home. He would eat things off the floor or out of the bin and from outside. I could have no clutter on my sides as he would eat whatever it was - money, rubbish or even a mobile phone. Kai started to eat the gravel we had out in the garden, so we had to turf and get rid of it all. Then he turned his attentions to the bark that was under his special swing, he ate it and sucked it and no matter how many times I grabbed it off him he would find more. He ended up in hospital after eating bark, he had a reaction to the dye that was in it so we had to stay in whilst he was observed. He came up in a huge rash all over his body, so we had to get rid of the bark.

When Kai went back to school I got a phone call a few weeks later, he was playing outside and he grabbed a mushroom from the garden that had been missed...but not by Kai! And ate it. Another hospital trip where we were in for over eight hours in the poison unit so they could find out what mushroom it was. The school were so apologetic and the head even met me at the hospital and stayed with me a while, but it wasn't their fault, Kai is so quick no one stands a chance!

Another time he went in a drawer and found a pack of those glow sticks that were all the rage. I had brought them for him so we could sit in the dark and look at the colours. Well, he opened the pack with his teeth and drank the fluid in the tubes. I walked in the room and saw three tubes he had eaten and was horrified, so back to the hospital with another eight hours in the poison unit! Kai was climbing on everything so we had to have everything minimal, I even caught him trying to hang from the mirror on the wall once. We had to move the front room around so he had nothing to get to it by climbing! He climbed over the fence, so we had to 6ft fence it the whole way around with gates with padlocks.

His balance was becoming a major issue, he was so unsteady and the stairs were a nightmare with them, he would try to walk up there backwards or down on one leg with his eyes closed. He would try to jump off the steps or sometimes miss a few steps altogether! We ended up in hospital twice where he fell down and hurt his head. Kai has always been big for his size and I just couldn't carry him up there, it was killing my back so I got onto social services. I explained he needed a downstairs bedroom as the stairs were a real issue for both of our safety. It was arranged that they would come out for the day to observe Kai, after half an hour they said they had enough evidence on Kai to show we were in need of a down stairs room. So much for a whole day, Kai had managed to fit every stunt he knew into thirty minutes!

It was a long process as the social services would have to present their case and apply for a disability grant through the council. Lots of meetings would have to take place and if and when it was accepted they would need to come out a few times to measure and draw up plans we were all happy with and then go back to go over them. Then they would need to apply for all of the resident's permission and the parish council to see if there were any objections to an extension going up, then they would have to hire the people, release the money and then start. So it would take a good year or so just to start it! They had given us options first before they could ask for a grant. I was told I had to show willing to move and look around at least 2-3 houses. I refused, I was not willing to move at all, why should we? Kai was settled we had made our home safe for him, we had a downstairs toilet and bathroom and had spent hundreds of pounds decorating and making it all safe. There was no way we could afford to move and start over again, and I wasn't going to unsettle and uproot

Kai or Bailey. I fought hard for that grant and argued that if I were to put Kai into care it would cost *them* thousands of pounds a week, we were asking for a grant to give Kai an extra room so we could keep him at home with us forever. In effect we were saving them money! It must have hit a nerve as I wasn't asked to look around any homes after my argument and the grant was approved! We won.

Around this time Scott and I decided that we were in such a happy place we would like to try for another baby, well it was more Scott going on and on about how broody he was! So I came off the contraceptive pill. Things were going right for a change, Kai hadn't had a seizure in months and now the extension was approved, it would make our lives so much easier. The safe space was a godsend and the room would be made big enough to accommodate that for Kai. We went over the plans as every last detail had to be written down and measured. It was explained that the whole kitchen would have to be ripped out and started again as the window and the door would need completely relocating. Typical really as we had only just had the kitchen done the previous year! I was asked if I needed a wet room as the outhouse building outside that they were going to knock down had a toilet in it and it wouldn't cost them extra as the plumbing was already there. I refused, Kai wouldn't need a wet room he could get in and out of the bath with help so I felt it was a waste of time. When they left Scott and Beckie sat me down and explained he would get bigger and harder to lift and manage. I knew they were right but a wet room was scary, it was like accepting he would one day need things like a wheelchair, and as crazy as it sounds I wasn't ready to face any of that. I rang them back and explained yes, we would like a wet room and the poor guy had to come back out the following week, sit down and go back over the plans. He said we would need a hallway, a wet room and a bedroom with wider doors for the future.

I was thinking we needed a holiday so I thought we should book one for the following summer, I rang Beckie and just mentioned it to her. "Well before you go booking anything don't you think you should do a pregnancy test first?"

I hadn't even thought of that as my period was due any day, but said I would to put her mind at rest. Scott was lying in the bath and I went in and peed on the white stick explaining that Beckie had banned me from booking a holiday until I knew if I was pregnant and although I didn't feel I was, I would just do it to shut her up. As I carried on chatting to him I left the stick on the toilet and flushed the chain and washed my hands, I turned back and there was two lines in the window. I stared at it in shock.

"I'm pregnant!" I said to Scott. Of course, he was over the moon and jumped out of the bath excitedly. I rang Beckie to tell her. "I'm going to be a nanny again," she said. Bailey had started to call her Nan from around eight months and it stuck ever since! *Lucky I didn't book that holiday!*

My nan had now been back and forth to the hospital, her back had crumbled and now her kidneys were failing due to the medication she was on at that time. She now had to go in three to four times a week to have dialysis and she was extremely fed up. We

128

managed to go and visit her, and I explained about the extension being built so we would have a wet room for her to use when she came to visit, but she turned to me and said, "Vikki, I can't, I have to have this every week without fail." It was then that I realised just how bad my nan's health had declined over the last year or so. It broke my heart as I loved her visits, she would come down and stay for the weekend and we would go to the car boot sale and sit up late watching a film. But still I thought she will be fine, look how much she has gone through and how hard she has fought, she is going nowhere!

The pregnancy was horrendous it was so different to the boys' ones, everyone said it would be a girl, but I wasn't convinced. Scott longed for a girl but didn't want to get his hopes up so we thought of boys names. I was sick from the minute I got up until the minute I went to bed, anything would set me off, but the main thing I couldn't stomach was anything wet. So I couldn't drink or eat anything like soup or sauce, I hated the smell of water (yes, I know, weird) and when I had a bath I would be throwing up in the sink at the fact it was touching me. Washing my hair was torture! I ended up on anti-sickness tablets and developed hyperemesis gravidarum, which is severe sickness.

Everything tasted disgusting, I would throw up brushing my teeth, and was getting no fluids in me at all. The doctor said I was dehydrated and would end up in hospital so I ate an ice pop and those little beauties became my life saver! I would go through boxes of 30 a day, and ice, I would crunch it so it didn't melt in my mouth. I lost a lot of weight and didn't really show until I was around seven months pregnant. Kai would lay his head on my tummy as if he knew, and be shocked when he felt a little kick. Bailey was now just over two and Kai loved him, he now acknowledged him, I think it was because Bailey would bring him half eaten biscuits or soggy crisps or his juice cup. Kai realised he was useful after all. Bailey would mimic Kai's rocking and noises and flapping of his hands, he would also get frustrated that Kai wouldn't play with him, but over time started to understand that he *couldn't* rather than *wouldn't*. They used to cuddle up on the sofa, Kai's head on Bailey's and fall asleep; it was lovely to see the bond forming between them both.

The doctor said he thought I was having a girl as the pregnancy was so different to the previous two, my body was reacting totally different this time. He was proved right at my five month scan; we couldn't believe it when the sonographer said, "Would you like to know the sex of the baby?"

Scott could barely contain his excitement. "Yes!" he nearly shouted in excitement.

When she said the words, "It's a girl." Scott burst into tears and so did I. It was the cherry on the cake as she was perfectly healthy with no signs of TS, and I felt good with no bad feelings. We wouldn't have cared if it was a little boy. We now just had the fight over names! I had chosen both of the boys' names so had stupidly said Scott could choose this baby's name as I thought it would be a boy! Now it was a girl I wanted to pick it! But Scott was having none of it. He liked the name Honey which I actually didn't like it on its own, but he was adamant that was the name he wanted. So I added the name Mae, she would also have my nan's name as a middle name, Patricia. Honey-Mae Patricia Hammond, I liked it. I also developed SPD, which is pelvic pain in pregnancy and it was agony to even open my legs or lay down, get up etc. Emotionally, I felt great though, no more dark clouds, Kai was over the worst and the operations were a distant memory, but physically I was fed up!

I had brought everything pink, from dummies to the pram! I was *so* over the colour blue, everything now had to be pink. I also kept having strange dreams. I would dream the date 12th and convinced myself this was when Honey-Mae would be born, I mentioned the date to Beckie and Scott and thought no more of it.

I got a phone call one afternoon out of blue whilst in the garden with Scott, Beckie and the boys, it was my biological dad, Darren, and I instantly knew something was wrong. "Vikki, I have really bad news. Nan is in a bad way, you need to come down and see her today, she isn't going to make it."

I was stunned, yes, I knew she was ill but she had always fought it off. I just couldn't take in what was being said to me at all. He was crying and so was I, I thought he had made a mistake or maybe it was a scare and she would surprise us like she had in the past. I was in a real state but Beckie took hold of me by the shoulders and said, "Go! You need to be with your nan, I'll have the boys." Scott and I ran inside to get changed, neither of us could believe it. Ten minutes ago we were sitting in the blazing sun watching the boys run around the garden and now we were going to travel to London to say goodbye to my nan. It didn't make sense.

I rang my dad, Darren, back and he explained that Granddad was phoning everyone but he couldn't bring himself to phone me, so my dad did. He said Nan had gone in as normal for her dialysis and they couldn't find a way to get in, and the only option was an operation, which she refused. She had had enough of fighting and of being in constant pain and of hospitals, I was shocked and in my selfish head I wanted her to have the operation so she could stay with us. She was only sixty-one, no age at all, I wasn't ready to let her go, not yet. She was the one I rang to confide in, the one I rang when Kai proved us all wrong with his walking. She was the one I leant on when I needed support, she had been there from day one and always phoned me and I used to go and see. We were very close, I was like her daughter and she was like a mum to me. I couldn't lose her; she wouldn't get to see the baby, and with my mum gradually declining, Nan was the one person I could rely on.

The drive there was slow, although I was dreading getting to the hospital I knew I would live to regret it if I didn't go. Everyone was carrying on with their day, rushing around, browsing in the shops, on their phone or waiting for a bus. I wanted to scream at them all - didn't they know what was happening? Why was everything still normal when all I could feel was this ball of pain in my tummy? Scott was heartbroken too, he adored my nan and was close to her too. She used to treat him to little gifts and he would tell her off for spending her money on him.

We pulled up to the hospital and my dad met us outside.

"I have to warn you, she is in a really bad way," he said. I could see his eyes were red and it hit me this was real, there was no mistake, this was it our final goodbye.

I entered the room and she was lying in a bed in the corner, she was very high on the drugs they had given her. My granddad came over and we hugged for a long time, he looked broken. I walked over to my nan, she looked so frail, not at all like the strong women we all knew.

As I held her hand she said, "I'm sorry, Vikki, I really am but you have to stay strong for the baby." I tried to hold back the tears but it was no use, my body heaved and I was shaking with the pain screaming inside me. I put my head near hers. "Don't you cry, don't do this to me, I can't see you cry." I held back the rest of my tears and she said, "I love you, I'm so proud of you." She looked past me to Scott and nodded her head and smiled. I could see Scott's eyes filling up with tears as my granddad sat with his head in his hands and my dad was looking anywhere but at us.

"I love you so much, Nan, thank you for everything." I sat holding her hand and the drugs started to kick in, she was moaning in pain and hallucinating.

"Ice cubes, they are the most simple things, my mouth was dry and the nurses put an ice cube on my lips, magic," she was mumbling to herself, her eyes were closed as she talked. We sat there, all of us together, united in grief as we watched the most

133

amazing person ebbing away in front of us. Finally it was time to go, and I gave her a last kiss on her cheek and held onto her hand. "I love you," I said and walked away. I couldn't look back.

The next few days passed and each day I would phone for an update to how she was, and she was still the same so I began to hope. Maybe she would win this battle too? I just couldn't comprehend life without Nanny Pat in it. I had so many memories of us going to Butlins, just the two of us watching Elvis shows. Going to Thorpe Park with the nursery and I insisted on one last walk along the beach, we lost track of time and missed the coach home. London dungeons and the Tower of London, sitting in the Wimpy for a sneaky burger and a knickerblockerglory, and walking around to the Christmas shop in the summer to buy Christmas decorations! I guess that's where my passion for Christmas comes from. She was young at heart and I used to live across the road from her right up until I was eleven and would see her all of the time.

I went to bed one night and was in a deep sleep when I felt Scott sit on the bed and noticed the lamp was on, I knew he wouldn't wake me up for no reason as it took me ages to get to sleep with the big bump I now had. "Your dad just rang."

I looked at him confused and then I knew instantly what he was going to say. "Don't say it!" I cried.

He took me in his arms. "She's gone, Vikki, she's free from pain."

I sobbed on his shoulder for so long, I had no tears left to cry. I looked at the clock, it was gone midnight. She died on the 12th June, my dreams now made sense. They were giving me the date my nan would die, not the date my daughter would be born.

The funeral was hard; there were so many people at the funeral, hundreds, so lot's had to stand outside. Even her nurses came, she was a special lady my nan, with a heart of gold, and it was a comfort to see so many people felt the same.

Seeing her coffin walked down the aisle was surreal. I just couldn't believe she was gone. It wasn't until my little sister, Katie, stood up in front of everyone and did a reading that I lost it, as did everyone else. There were so many flowers even though her wish was for no flowers, just donations to breast cancer, she still got a load. The gathering afterwards was at her local pub, and everyone had a story to tell or to share, it was lovely to hear so many nice things. I couldn't stay long, being in that pub without her felt wrong. I just wanted to get home to my babies. Scott was amazing those next few months, it took me a very long time to come to turns with it. Because she'd lived in London, a fair few miles from me, I would kid myself that she was still there. I kept her number on my phone for years after and would call it just to hear the voice message. But after so long, the line went dead and I couldn't call it anymore.

It was a weird few weeks leading up to the birth I was excited to meet my daughter but heartbroken my nan wouldn't get to meet her. It was around this time I started paying an interest in the afterlife - it was a comfort to think she was still there and not just *gone*. I went to a charity night hosted by

135

a psychic called Donna Fallon. I instantly loved her; she was spot on and had a way about her that made me want to listen to her all day. She then started saying the name Pat, and I realised this was for me! She said to look for butterfly signs (another friend who was psychic had recently said the same). She told me it was her breast area that there was a problem, and also that she was very swollen and bloated at the end and couldn't walk. She gave me a lovely message from Nanny Pat and everything she said was spot on. It comforted me knowing this, and Donna would later become one of the people that would help heal me in my tough times.

Our downstairs extension finally got the go ahead, and we were give the date of the beginning of August, the baby was due the end of July so this would mean a hell of bad timing but we needed it done urgently for Kai as his climbing and lack of coordination were becoming a major issue. Around this time he also managed to get out of the front door and was sitting in next door's driveway staring at their shiny car. I was terrified as we hadn't even realised he managed to get out so quickly! He was always making escape plans and we had to be so much more aware, it was like having a toddler but in a big boy's body!

He still hadn't had a seizure and was doing really well at school; he loved swimming and going on little trips out. He was learning so much more and started to say Dad again, a word we never thought we would hear again. Scott was so happy and hugged him tight, we had done the right thing after all, even though there were big setbacks and problems he had come through the other side. He was thriving and this was the best we had seen him in a very long time, although his behaviour was still up and down he now slept a lot better as he had the safe space. He had started to put his hand inside his nappy a lot more and this was becoming a major issue. I walked in his room one morning and was instantly hit with the smell of poo. As I unzipped his safe space I couldn't believe my eyes, he had pooped in his nappy and had smeared poo everywhere, walls, floor and bedding were covered in it. His face, nails and legs were smeared too. Scott got to work cleaning up the mess as I could barely bend down with the bump, I had to put Kai in the bath. Which to him was a big reward and he happily giggled and splashed away delighted he had got a treat. I had to throw away all of his bedding and the house stank of bleach. We now had to work out how to stop him getting into his nappy, and started to buy special all-in-one vests that buttoned over his nappy. Once his clothes were on he couldn't get down there, we also brought all in one pyjamas as onesies were yet to make a comeback. It worked for a while but then Kai realised he could get through the side of his vest and into his nappy that way! So we tried shorts under his vest, again he pulled them aside. Then I came up with a great idea... leotards! From the local dance shop they did full length ones that came over the feet. Once his t-shirt was on he couldn't get down there at all, as he can't undress himself.This idea was great and he still has to wear them to this day as he thinks nothing of playing with himself in public!

The midwife came to give me a sweep one afternoon as I was now five days over my due date and a complete misery. I was eating a cream apple cake when she came so I left it on the side and went upstairs for my sweep. Beckie and Scott were playing in the garden with the boys.

As she was in the middle of the sweep she looked concerned and said, "Are you in any pain?"

I was now also worried and answered, "Only a little bit, on and off for the past week or so."

Her eyes widened. "You are seven centimetres dilated! Your waters are bulging and you need to go to the hospital now." I calmly got dressed and asked her to tell Scott as I knew he would panic and he was more than likely to stay calm with her. As I came downstairs she was just leaving and wished me luck. I walked into the kitchen and continued eating my cake as I walked into the garden. Beckie was on the phone and Scott was running backwards and forwards in a flap. I am not kidding, it was like a scene from a cartoon he was in a real state of panic and didn't know what to do! I sat down watching the drama.

"Vikki, quick get your stuff you have to go now!" Beckie shouted.

"Let me finish eating my cake first," I said.

She looked at me in shock."You can take your effing cake with you! The midwife said if your waters break the baby will be here!"

Scott came running over. "I'll go get the bags! Shit we have no petrol in the car! Come on why are you still sitting there, let's go!"

As soon as I got into the car I started having contractions. We got to the hospital and the lady was just going to send me to the ward when I announced, "The midwife rang ahead as I'm seven centimetres dilated."

She looked at me shocked and directed us upstairs to the labour ward. I felt so guilty walking past all those mums on the ward straight to the room every pregnant lady longs to be. The midwife that introduced herself had two butterfly tattoos on her wrist and I instantly remembered what Donna had said and I felt at ease. Contractions were coming but my waters wouldn't budge so they broke them for me and instantly the action started. The contractions came thick and fast and there was no time for pain relief only gas and air.

As I was giving my final pushes Scott said, "Look over there." Sitting on the window outside was a pure white butterfly. Honey-Mae came screaming into the world on the 31st July 2008 weighing 8Ib 14ozs, Scott was instantly in love and couldn't stop cuddling her. As soon as I held her I also fell in love, she had blue eyes, blonde hair and my nan's nose. I checked straight away to make sure she was a girl as I still couldn't believe it! After a few minutes I was given an injection to help my placenta come along. Honey-Mae was downing milk and crying for more, when the midwife said the placenta wasn't coming. I had to wait to see if it would, but as time went on the pain was horrendous and it actually felt like I was in labour all over again! They tried to pull the cord but felt it would snap, so they put me on a drip to kick start the contractions to make the placenta come. But again nothing, by this point I was screaming in pain and Scott was left holding the baby whilst I was rushed to theatre. They made me sign some consent forms and then gave me a spinal block and manually removed the placenta, as I was laying there the pain went away instantly. I could see a pair of legs in the air. It was bizarre when I realised they were my legs! I was numb from the shoulders down and it made me panic as I couldn't move, but I calmed myself down in time to be wheeled to Scott. He was worried sick as he thought I was going to die, it affected him for a very long time after, he said being left with a new baby and not knowing what was going on was hell.

We took Honey-Mae home and Kai wasn't impressed at all, he sat with his fingers in his ears as if to say 'really another one?!' Bailey was a bit put-out too, he was used to not sharing as Kai didn't want what he had unless it was food, and I think Bailey realised this baby would be different!

The extension work started when Honey-Mae was three days old. It was chaos as it was the six weeks school holiday so I had the boys at home too. Workmen would come at eight in the morning and leave at four in the afternoon, there was dust and mess everywhere… and the noise! The garden was completely out of bounds as they had to lay the foundations, the kitchen was ripped apart so I had everything in my front room and Kai was in his element as it was easy access to food!

Honey-Mae was such a happy, contented baby, always happy to lay there and look around. I had felt no worries about her at all and felt great in myself, things were finally starting to work out. Scott and I were great, we talked to each other about our feelings more now the operations were over with. The boys were bonding more each day and Bailey was so good with Kai, the house was now getting sorted so it would be safe for Kai. It was just a hole left in my heart where my nan once was.

Kai's pram was now getting too small and I just assumed he would need a bigger one, looking back I was stupid to think that as a Maclaren major is pretty damn big! We went to his appointment and were offered a wheelchair. I was horrified, I thought back to the holiday in Wales with Jake when we both thought that Kai would never need a wheelchair. I don't know why I had such a big issue, but I felt in my heart like it was admitting defeat and taking a step back. I had always thought, over time, Kai would get steadier and maybe now his seizures had stopped he would walk a bit more, but it was becoming obvious he couldn't. Also with his escape plans there wasn't many more options left, and so he was measured and tried them all out.

Kai loved the wheelchair, though; it was bigger, comfier and better for him, he kept going back to sit in it and didn't want to leave it alone! I knew this was the right thing to do but I still shed a few tears to myself thinking of yet another milestone lost. It was also around this time that my mum now needed a wheelchair; her balance was poor, as was her coordination, she would also wander off so it was safer for her to be in a chair. She could still talk and would abuse Scott on a regular basis and loved it when he abused her back. She was obsessed with my dad and wouldn't leave him alone!

141

I decided with the extension going on and being stuck in a lot to send Kai to a half term club especially designed for special needs. As anyone who knows me will know this was a tough decision as I hate him not in my sight, but felt it would be good for him to be mixing. There was a local one about fifteen minutes' drive from me and a lot of the staff from his school worked there, so I trusted them. It was around eight pounds a day and I put him in three times a week, it had a garden and bouncy castle and lots of activities. There are not many facilities for the disabled and clubs and things are scarce. Kai didn't like it and cried a lot, this was mainly my fault because he is only used to being with me and I am not used to letting him go. After only two weeks of trying, I gave up. He hasn't been to anything like it since.

It's sad really but there is a real lack of any sort of play scheme for the disabled. Unless you want respite you are limited to anything else, I have had no family support worker and left without consultants and some points, no epilepsy nurse and no help from social services as they keep swapping over social workers. I am lucky to have Beckie and Scott and of course Kai is at school five times a week which gives me time to clean and organise the kids. It is scary looking to the future and I never do, as I worry about what will happen when Kai leaves school and when he is discharged from Great Ormond Street, which is a children's hospital and into a normal hospital as, with my mum, I felt the care was not as good.

There are a lot of questions, Kai will get bigger, stronger and heavier as the years go by and I want him at home with me until the day I'm too ill or old to care for him. But what then? I often get asked these questions but I have no answers as I just don't know! One of the worst things I have had said to me was this: "What will happen if you die before Kai?"

I was shocked as I hadn't really given it much thought. "I don't know," I muttered.

Then they continued and said, "Hopefully he will die before you and you won't have that worry."

I was shocked and this comment stayed with me for a long time and cut deep, the person that said it wasn't being spiteful, it was a genuine question, but it hurt and made me think about that for a long time. The thing I find with having a disabled child is people feel they can ask what they want, which as I said earlier on I like questions I would rather that than stares, but I wish people would think before they ask one that can leave an imprint on you.

Unwanted advice is another one. People are quick to say if Kai was kicking off how to handle him or he shouldn't have a dummy, dip it in curry powder. If I felt I needed advice I would ask for it, otherwise don't offer it as it is very insulting! I didn't see the problem in Kai having a dummy aged four and a half, it was a comfort for him and after everything he had been through I felt he needed it. But going back to when he was five I had to take them away as he had started to put them in his mouth, the whole thing and it was becoming dangerous. He wasn't as bad as I thought he would be and coped well without them.

The extension was complete after a good nine months. It changed our lives completely. We had a bigger kitchen and a hallway that lead to a wet room and Kai's bedroom. All on ground level, no more stairs! His safe space was put in there from upstairs and it had room for a sofa bed which we could sleep on if he had a bad night, he could also sit on it with his patio doors open to look into the garden - which also meant he could go outside and in whenever he needed to. He had space for his toys and we also applied to a charity for sensory lights which was accepted. He had a bubble tube and projector and string lights which he loves. It has opened up a whole new world for him and has allowed him to be more independent as he can choose if he wants to go outside play with his toys or lights or just sit on his sofa and chill out. It also gave him somewhere to go if it was too noisy for him in the front room with Honey-Mae and Bailey crawling and running about. It has made our lives so much different and we are able to care for Kai the way he deserves to be cared for. We moved Honey-Mae into Kai's old room so they now had a room each, but we both started to get very broody!

CHASING SHADOWS

After a content three years of Kai at his best we were the happiest we ever had been and then we had the date to go for Kai's kidney scan. I had a bad feeling and voiced my concerns to both Beckie and Scott. I took Kai for his scan and he lay there contentedly, hands down his pants, then fell asleep and started snoring. I guess it was the dark room and the hum of the machine! As she started the scan I noticed a few lumps that were there before and then noticed she was measuring and re-measuring and my heart sank. I knew I was right whenever I felt this feeling I now knew to trust it. I didn't need to wait for the results Kai's kidney lumps had grown and the results a week later confirmed it. I felt sick to my stomach. After everything else, this felt like a punch in the gut. When would my boy get a break?

Although they were not big enough to cause concern he now had to have yearly kidney scans to keep an eye on them. He had also started to sign 'thank you' and more at school, he would sign more at home but never thank you! Little monkey was always making me work for his response.

Honey-Mae was now two and running around with Bailey. Kai had just started to acknowledge Honey-Mae as she was now at the age where she was useful to him, he would sit while she played mum to him, feeding him her food and sharing her drinks. She now had a purpose and he would tap her on the head in appreciation. Honey-Mae was the double for my Nan who I missed so much, I started to go and see Donna more as it gave me comfort to hear from my nan. Donna told me that she could see blood tests and an operation for Kai in the future. She said we faced tough times but we would get through it. She also said I would be writing something which I never thought I would, and yet here I am!

She then turned to me and said, "You have two boys and two girls, don't you?"

I replied, "Donna, you know I have two boys and one girl."

She looked straight at me and then stated, "I can clearly see a little girl that is already here, you are pregnant."

I was stunned, I had come off the pill the month before and me and Scott had kept it quiet just telling Beckie as we thought it may take a while. But there was no way I could be pregnant yet it was too soon surely, I still had a week until my period was due so wouldn't know until then.

A week later I urinated on the white stick and straight away two lines started to appear, Donna was

146

right, I was pregnant! As the weeks went on I felt more and more sick, worse than with Honey-Mae. I couldn't eat or keep fluid down and ice pops made me feel worse. The only thing the baby liked was slush puppies, not easy to get in Hitchin! I was put on anti-sickness tablets and it was such a high dosage that as soon as the kids were asleep I would crawl into bed and sleep soundly until the next morning and be tired all day long! I knew there and then it was a girl, Donna was right! The scan confirmed we were having a healthy little girl, we were over the moon our family was now complete. After this pregnancy I certainly didn't want anymore.

I developed SPD again and lifting and changing Kai was hard work and completely took it out of me. He has always been big for his age, sturdy and tall, and sometimes very unhelpful and uncooperative.

Kai became unwell the next few days, as did the other two, and merely days later he came out in spots - chicken pox! I was now five months pregnant and had to go and have a blood test to see if I had it as it wasn't on my records, as it turned out I didn't and had to go straight to the hospital. I had to have the biggest injection I had ever seen into the top of my arm which swelled up like a balloon! I was just thankful the baby would be OK, and then Bailey and Honey-Mae got it, too. It was a fun few weeks I can tell you!

After the chicken pox saga had ended, Kai then came down with a big red rash all up his back and side. I took him to the doctors as he was crying in pain when I changed his nappy which was so unlike

Kai he rarely cried. He had shingles! My poor boy I couldn't believe it! He was in a lot of pain those next few days and would curl up on a ball and rock, it was heart-breaking to see.

A few weeks later I was bathing Kai and I slipped in the bathroom and did the splits and with SPD it was agony! I was all right and didn't fall so didn't think anymore of it until the next day when I went to the toilet and saw blood. I was now seven months pregnant and blood was pouring out of me so I was rushed to hospital. I was terrified I was going to lose the baby I had already bonded with and was scanned and monitored and kept in overnight. Thankfully, the baby was fine, but I bled for weeks afterwards and it was so upsetting seeing so much blood. Scott and Beckie wouldn't let me lift or deal with Kai at all after that, and it really upset me. As much as I knew they were right I was aching to just help him and he sometimes played Scott up as he wanted me to dress him! I felt helpless as I was used to doing everything for Kai, obviously Scott and Beckie also helped but having a complete ban was hard on us both, but I reasoned it wouldn't be forever just a few more weeks.

I was thoroughly fed up by now, and had managed to get the midwife to sweep me at dead on 40 weeks, as I just wanted to feel back to normal and be able to care for Kai again. She took pity on me and gave me a thorough sweep, it can take up to forty eight hours to work and I was coming up to this now and still nothing. I lay on the sofa all day and didn't move once. Scott took the kids to school whilst I felt totally miserable! He also picked them up and went off to work whilst I fed, bathed and put them to bed, then I lay back on the sofa, glum.

Scott come back home later that night. "Are you still feeling sorry for yourself? Come on we will go upstairs on the computer and put some things on eBay that will cheer you up."

Yes, I'm sure that really bloody would I thought and followed him up, as I started walking up each step I felt something weird between my legs and got to the top of the landing and dropped my trousers. Scott looked on bemused and suddenly my waters went and gushed down my legs.

Scott looked horrified. "You're wetting yourself!"

I grinned. "No I'm not, my waters have just gone!" This was it, finally the day had come to meet our baby.

Beckie's mum, Dot, sat with the kids as this time Beckie wanted to be there to see the birth, as soon as I got to hospital my contractions stopped and after waiting until 1am Beckie and Scott went home and I was going to be induced in the morning. I woke at 6am to my belly tightening and was led into the labour room where things moved quickly, before I knew it I was on gas and air as Beckie and Scott arrived. It was a very calm labour, I had an epidural and felt nothing, completely pain free! I could still feel pressure and after a few pushes Daisy Florence arrived into the world on the 31st March 2011.

She was beautiful she looked just like Scott, his nose and eyes but with blonde hair. She weighed 8lb 1oz and we were allowed to take her home the day after. Introducing her to Kai was the same as usual, he didn't even look her way, just at me as if to say 'really another one?' We gave her the middle name Florence after Scott's Nan who died a few years before. She was an easy baby and sucked her thumb from day one, so if she cried I'd go to get her a bottle and come back and she would have her thumb in her mouth fast asleep!

Kai was doing so well on his feet that he had started to do horse riding with his school, something I would never have dreamed would be possible before as he was so unpredictable, but he had calmed a lot and seemed to enjoy the motion of the trot and pace of the horse. He was doing well at school and his seizures were still under complete control. He was giving amazing eye contact and had even started to call out "Beck" For Beckie. We were over the moon and he used this word to his full advantage leading her to the bath and shouting Beck as he didn't want a shower!

I should have known things were going too well, we weren't used to being so happy, and it all came crashing down one afternoon.

Kai was sitting on the sofa and I glanced up and saw what I thought to be the end of a seizure, I couldn't be certain as it was a few seconds, but in my heart I just knew they were back. I felt deflated. The thing with TS that makes the condition so cruel is it is so unpredictable, you are lured into a false sense of security and then bam, something happens to bring you back to earth with a bump. I mentioned to Scott that I thought it was a seizure and we kept a close eye on him hoping I was wrong.

The next day we both saw him have one and it took all my energy not to cry. He had had nearly four year's seizure free and I was so happy as he had come such a long way. He had learnt new skills and was always up to no good, the best he had ever been. I know it must have felt very strange for Kai having no seizures as he was so used to having up to twenty a day, so to go to none must have been very odd to him especially as we had no way of explaining to him. I was hoping it was just a couple and he was maybe brewing an illness and he seemed OK for the next few weeks. Then his behaviour completely changed, it was the worst six week holiday than ever before. He was climbing again and very destructive, he would walk into the kitchen and throw glass across the floor to hear the sound. We had to come back from our holiday early as he was smashing his head off the walls and making the caravan rock, it was like he had the devil in him. As horrible as it sounds, I longed for the nights so I could put him to bed and relax without fear of him hurting himself or breaking something.

He broke our tumble dryer, a brand new phone and numerous cups, glasses and plates. He started to be quite spiteful and pulled your hair and started to bite, especially if you had your back to him. He would pull your face to face him and then try to bite or pull your hair for that extra bit of attention and then laugh once he had got it. If we ignored him he would do it harder and shout. I was pulling my hair out wondering what the sudden change in him was, but it all started to make sense once September came.

151

Kai's seizures had started to come back and they were worse than ever before, so far he was having around three a day, but they would be full on drop attacks, he would fall straight to the floor with no warning at all. He would bang his head, face, elbows and legs with a hard thud as his body made contact with the floor. We couldn't let him in the kitchen on his own as it was a tiled floor. Before, when he had seizures, we would get a little pre-warning a seizure was going to occur so could make him safe, now there was none.

Kai's seizures coming back was obviously quite new for the kids to witness and it really had an effect on them, but mainly on Bailey. They would all be eating breakfast at the table and Kai would suddenly fall forward and smash his face into his plate cutting all his lip and tongue, the site of all the blood horrified Bailey and he was very upset. Bailey had started to feel a real anger as he was at the age where he wanted to know about Kai. I had never really given it a second thought about how it would affect the kids, but now I felt pure guilt. Bailey wanted to know why his brother was poorly. Why he was in a wheelchair, but he could walk. Why he had seizures. Why couldn't he play with him and his toys? Why couldn't Kai talk? And why was he still in nappies? What would happen when he was older? And the one that hurt the most, why was Kai born like this, but he himself was all right? This question angered him a lot, he just couldn't understand why they were born so different and he felt a sense of guilt about it.

I sat him down and explain in the easiest way I could that Kai was born poorly, he had lumps in his head that stopped him speaking. It also stopped him being able to know how to play or go to the toilet, the lumps also caused him to have these seizures. I told him Kai would hopefully learn through all of us to say a new word or to sit for a short period and play in his own way. To explain why this had happened to him I had no answer, but had to try as this little boy in front of me was waiting for an explanation. Kai was born special, some children are born without their vision or hearing or without an arm or a leg. No one knew *why* it was just one of those things.

One day, while I was driving, Bailey said, "Mum, we are really lucky to have Kai in our life. Those who haven't got a brother with a lump in his head will never know what it feels like will they, Mum? We are very lucky." My eyes filled with tears and at that point I knew Bailey knew exactly why we were given Kai, he was teaching us a different world, a world not many were blessed to live in.

I was given a poem by Lyndsey at work a few years back and it really explains how it feels to have a disabled child, it has stayed with me and I highly recommend looking it up online. It is called Welcome to Holland by Emily Perl Kingsley.

Kai's seizures continued to gradually get worse; he was now having over thirty a day, all aggressive, and most left him injured. As time went on he started to have longer seizures lasting over five minutes, and had a big one at school lasting ten. I had never been scared of a seizure before as it was all I knew, but these were something else entirely. I would hold him in my arms on the floor willing them to stop before five minutes came up and he would have to have his rescue medicine. Every second that passed was pure agony, you feel nothing but useless when your child is thrashing about in your arms looking terrified and there is nothing you can do to stop it. He had started to go blue in the lips too which meant he was losing oxygen, this scared me a lot. The school decided that he would now have to travel to school in his wheelchair as it was too dangerous for him to walk onto the bus and sit in a normal seat. We had to go back to the wheelchair service and get a bigger wheelchair that reclined so if he had a seizure he could still breathe and get air instead of being slumped forward. This was great but caused a problem for us as we had a normal car that barely fitted his wheelchair in the boot. We were due to upgrade our car around this point as it is a disability car that Kai pays for out of his disability living allowance money. The school advised it would be better to apply for a bigger car, more like a bus, so Kai could be wheeled on like he is at school. This sounds really silly but I was in floods of tears phoning up to enquire about a wheelchair access vehicle. They were lovely though, and said we would qualify, but it felt like we were taking a giant step backwards.

I just didn't want to accept that his seizures were back, and I really didn't want him in his wheelchair as much as he would have to be. It felt like I was giving up on him, accepting that this was what life was going to be like. It's funny how a bit of equipment of car can affect you so much, I really don't know why, but to me it feels like steps back when I wanted Kai to be going forward. One of the worst comments I had was because of Kai's DLA car, someone once said that I was lucky to get a free car and they wish they could. Really? *Lucky*. One word I wouldn't use. I would never get to see my child marry or have children, never get to hear him say "I love you Mummy." Never get to see my child be seizure free, and have to constantly worry about his future. I would need to be there for him twenty-four hours a day, seven days a week for the rest of my life, changing his nappy, feeding him, bathing him and being his voice. I don't call that lucky at all, as for it being 'free' it isn't, it is paid for out of Kai's DLA money. Having an adapted car so you can wheel you child into it in their wheelchair so they can be sat upright so they don't slump forward and stop breathing, hardly luck is it? I would gladly hand the car back if I could swap it for a little normality. Funny thing was, she was the lucky one she just couldn't see it.

We were referred back to Great Ormond Street Hospital. It was like going back all those years. It felt wonderful to have been signed off, like we were looking forward, now it felt like we were back to that dark place I never wanted to be in again. I had sworn Kai would never have another operation, the last one had taken it out on him and all of us. It was tough on him and us, as a family and I had just about come through it. We had options and for that I will always be grateful, at least we could rule things out or try something instead of having to just accept that this is it.

Again the VNS was mentioned, as was a new drug trial everolimus and surgery, this time a corpus callosotomy. First Kai would need the never ending tests to see if he was eligible for surgery. The drug trial was a new thing and I had lost confidence in any medication. It had made him grumpy or sleep too much or not at all, it had made him gain weight or lose weight, or be hyperactive. I had had enough of Kai being a guinea pig and although I hated the thought of yet more surgery we were running out of options. With the last surgery he had had a good few years grace from having seizures and he had come a long way. Over the next year and a half he had a week's stay for a telemetry and more MRI and other scans, more appointments and more hospital stays.

In these moments I wished Kai could talk to help me decide with him. I felt like I was taking his life in my hands every time I signed the consent forms and it made me feel incredibly guilty. Making the decisions for him was heart-breaking and also like taking a huge gamble, so much could go wrong, but then so much could go wrong if we left Kai the way he was now. There was another outbreak of chicken pox and all of my children got it again –yes, I know, unlucky! Kai was covered this time and he and Bailey had it first and then the girls. It was another month of illness and it was driving me insane. Just as things were getting back to normal, Kai again got shingles. I felt like screaming. It was frustrating seeing him in so much pain time and time again. His immune system must have been very low as he got a few bugs over the next few months.

It was moments like this that I questioned myself, when he was at his lowest and having to deal with seizures as well as everything else. I would sit and think - did I do the right thing? In that I mean going ahead with the pregnancy. As shocking as this may sound it was how I felt. I wondered if I was too selfish to let him go, and instead he was facing a life time of pain and confusion because of my decision. Don't get me wrong, I loved Kai, illness and all, and wouldn't change him for the world, but it made me think how did HE feel?

Around this time I started seeing Donna more as I had seen a few signs - pure white feathers would appear from nowhere in my front room or bedroom, or fall outside at my feet. I believed they were a sign from above and Donna thought so too - from my Nan saying 'stay strong, stay standing, you can do this, don't fall.'

After a visit to Donna I was sitting thinking how I could raise money and awareness for the TS association, after all they had helped me in so many ways over the years. They had provided me with an advisor, Heather who I would call at night when I felt low and was full of questions about surgery. She even visited me at my home and also came to two hospital appointments with me to help me take in news. They had forwarded my details to a charity who gave us a wonderful holiday when we needed it the most. They also once gave us £200 towards a costly hospital stay, which meant Scott could afford to take time off work to be at our side. I wanted to give something back, so I rang Donna.

I felt cheeky but asked if she would possibly hold a charity event, a psychic night with all proceeds going to TSA, she agreed straight away, no hesitation, and said she would be honoured. So, with the help of Beckie, I got to work. She said she would do a cupcake stall, and got to work planning on making over one hundred cakes! I leaned on friends with a local business to donate raffle prizes and received tons of donations from a Wii computer, thanks to Beckie's friend, nail and hair vouchers, cake and gifts, and photo shoots. I got the tickets made and Beckie's partner designed and paid for them. I hired a hall which Scott paid for. After months of hard work dropping and sending, saving and organising we had sold over 130 tickets!

The night was a huge success. Donna was amazing, as usual, and she also donated her CDs to the raffle. There was a bar at the hall so it felt like a much needed night out! We were very emotional when we raised £1,700 for the charity. Over the next two years Donna, again, did the night free of charge, for which I would be eternally grateful for. She was now more well-known and was mixing with celebrities and on TV, and also doing a tour of theatres as well as travelling abroad. I couldn't believe she would still do the evenings for a little known about disease for a local family like us. She has a special place in my heart for everything she has done, although she probably has no idea how much. Thanks to her, over the years we have made nearly £6,000 for TSA.

Kai's kidney lumps had grown in size again, but again it wasn't a concern as they still weren't at a worrying size. Still I worried, I thought back to Kai's SEGA that had all of a sudden become a life threatening issue and it scared me. It was like he had these little ticking time bombs in his body that could go off at any point in time. Not knowing is the worst kind of pain as you worry for the sake of worrying. You are always left waiting for bad news, or sometimes good. But I am quite a negative person in the sense that I always think the worst and then I am not shocked. I brace myself for the worst scenario, it's a protection thing and although it drives everyone mad it's my way of coping. If it is positive news great, but I am not letting my guard down, not ever.

My mum's condition had started to gradually deteriorate; she was now in a wheelchair full-time and was having trouble swallowing her food. She would choke which scared my dad and brother on many occasions, her motions and movements were like she was constantly drunk and her speech was slurred to the point where only a few knew what she was saying. I still found it very hard to see her as every time I did it would make me realise I was a step closer to losing her. You only ever get one mum and I felt robbed of mine. She was obviously still here but she was like a shell of her former self. She was reliant on every need and that was hard to see considering how fiercely independent and head strong she once was. She would still get her own way and flick the finger at my dad and she could still say "Fuck off," Pretty clearly! But I felt we had missed out on so much over the years, as did the kids. Honey-Mae was

159

terrified of her which I think upset my dad; it must have been terribly hard for him to see that. She wouldn't come to see her and would hide. Bailey was more accepting, I would tell him she was like Kai but had got poorly over time instead of being born with it. Daisy didn't care, she was too young to understand.

I took a lot of advice over the next few months from my friends Beckie, Sarah, Riaand Corina and also my online friends who had similar experiences. I also got to meet one of the online friends and her daughter when we were staying in Great Ormond Street Hospital at the same time. I had become very close to a lady called Liz, whom I have never met, but always takes the time to ask how I am and give me her opinion. She will be a lifelong friend, even when I was considering writing this book she pushed me to do it when I felt like giving up. Speaking to other TS mums was very comforting as I knew they had, or were facing, similar challenges.

Beckie was expecting a baby boy any time now, she was due end of December and the date had come and gone. When she was finally induced, I got a phone call at gone midnight. She had given birth to her first baby boy, Jude, on the 21st January - exactly the same birthday as Kai. We shared everything but this really did mean a lot to us. I had told her the previous year I could see a boy and knew this was her baby I could see. I also refused to let her in the house unless she did a pregnancy test first, as illness was about and I didn't want her ill. She came out of the toilet shaking and crying so much she couldn't breathe. She was pregnant, "I told you," I said before cuddling her, "now go!"

Waiting for news of the operation, again I stopped eating as much and couldn't sleep, panic would rise in the pit of my stomach but I would force it to stay there. I wasn't doing this again. I was not going to let these panic attacks rule me and I pushed them aside.

The day came for the test results and it was then that I knew we had to decide if we felt this surgery would benefit Kai. After so much advice and searching the web for information on the operation, we both decided we had to try it for Kai's sake. We couldn't let his seizures get longer or stronger and we couldn't risk turning down an option that could be the answer, we had to try it. Dr Hank explained that Kai *was* eligible for the operation and if we decided to go ahead with it he would be willing to do it and put Kai on the waiting list. He talked us through the operation in detail. The corpus callosum is severed in order to stop epileptic seizures. Once cut, the brain has more difficulty sending messages between the hemispheres. It may not affect the frequency of seizures but he hoped it would stop the drop attacks. There were risks of course, 1% risk of death, 5% risk of weakness down one side that could be permanent, and 5% risk of infection. Although the risks were low they were still risks, but we had to try this for Kai's sake.

Kai went on the waiting list and more tests came through. We had to go to an all-day development check where every single detail about Kai was gone through. His skin shaegreen patches were looked at as were his white patches and also his now obvious facial rash. He was weighed, measured and they did many little tests to get a basic score of Kai's ability. It came back as between 6-11 months. It was a tiring, exhausting day and I felt rough anyway so gladly fell into bed and slept soundly that night.

I woke up with a very upset tummy and it continued for days after, so we were careful to have sex on day 7 after my last bought of illness. I didn't think much more it and life carried on, constant appointments and having my phone to hand for when the school rang to say that Kai had had yet another seizure. I was getting ready to go to the dentist with Scott one morning after dropping the kids at school and Daisy to playgroup, when it suddenly hit me - I was two days late for my period. I am always spot on, so straight away I thought shit. I went to the chemist on the way to the dentist and told Scott who was instantly excited, I felt dread. This could not have come at a worse time and I prayed to God I wasn't. I also had Donna's voice in my ear who had told me months before she saw one more baby, and I said "Donna, you are wrong, no more for us." She replied to be very careful as a baby was waiting for us.

When we arrived at the doctors, I checked in at reception, then went straight to the toilet stuffed it in my pocket and went and sat with Scott in the waiting room. We waited a few minutes and I pulled the test out - two lines. Instantly Scott was grinning from ear to ear, but I felt sick, I told him not to get his hopes up and to keep it to ourselves as the second line was only faint.

I went straight outside and rang Beckie. "I'm pregnant," I blurted out before she had the chance to speak.

"OK, are you happy?" she asked.

"I don't know, Beckie, it's bad timing, I don't think I am, the line is very faint and I need to do another test."

She paused and listened and said, "Vikki, you know as well as I do that a line is a line." I knew she was right but my head was spinning, and I also had a feeling that something would happen.

From the first day I found out I was pregnant I had terrible back ache to the point where I could barely sit up straight. Scott had told so many people I had no choice but to announce it early, especially after he had told the kids! I had cramping and funny pains too, which I had never had in pregnancy before. A few days later I was just putting Daisy's shoes on to take her to toddler group when I felt very wet in my knickers and ran to the toilet. As I wiped I studied the paper and there was a pink colour on the toilet paper. I knew in my gut I was losing the baby, I shouted to Scott and we both sat and waited. We didn't know what to do or say and when I went back to the toilet this time there was bright blood. I had lost the baby. I felt numb but Scott was instantly heartbroken as we made our way to the hospital, where it was confirmed there was no baby. We travelled back in silence. As we walked through the door the answer phone was flashing so I hit play.

"Hello this is a message for the parents of Kai Hammond, this is Great Ormond Street Hospital calling with an operation date of the 20th March

163

2012." I couldn't believe it, it was one week away to the day!

I burst into uncontrollable sobs that shook my whole body, and Scott cried with me. This was too much for one day. I had no time to take in the news that the baby I had just been getting used to the idea of was gone. I now had a week to prepare us all for surgery; the kids would need looking after, Scott would have to have time off work. Oh God, the kids, how could I tell them there was now no baby and, oh by the way, we were going into hospital in a week and Kai was going to be having a major operation. I text Beckie. I couldn't talk because I was in too much of a state. I felt pure guilt at that moment as my initial reaction had been that I didn't want this baby because it was the wrong time. Now it was gone - had I wished it away? Had someone up there been listening and taken the baby from me? just as we were getting excited. I felt stupid for telling everyone so soon. All I could think about was my boy having yet another operation, I didn't know where to start. Beckie rang straight back and I answered we both didn't say anything we just sobbed down the phone. She didn't need to ask me anything she knew how I felt, she knew what was going through my mind.

"I will sort the kids out, stop worrying about that, I will be over after work. I love you," She said.

"I love you too," I said back.

I text Ria asking if she would collect the kids from school for me as I couldn't face anyone. She didn't even reply, she came straight over and hugged me so tight, both silent. Scott was outside, he didn't know what to say or do, he was in his own world of

164

pain. The door went again and Dot, Beckie's mum came in cuddled me and went about cooking for the kids, washing up and making herself busy. I am so very lucky to have these amazing people in my life, they don't know but their actions that day saved me from falling all over again.

Scott took it harder, he couldn't talk through the tears, and all he kept saying was "What are we going to do?" I had no answers, but I knew it would be all right as we had each other. A white feather on the garage wall also confirmed my belief in this, we would stay strong.

Telling the kids was hard; I explained that the baby had stopped growing as it was the wrong time to be born as Kai needed me more at the moment. He was going into hospital next week to have one of his little lumps removed to help stop his fits. I would need them to be very good for Beckie and Dot and I would ring them every night. They just looked up with their innocent eyes and accepted what I was telling them. They were upset there was now no baby as they were excited, and asked, "Will the baby grow again after?"

I nodded, "Yes it will."

I knew we would one day have another baby as the empty feeling I felt now made me yearn. Scott was too scared to ask but I knew he was desperate for another one, and as I was adamant no more he felt like that was it. We had a week to organise ourselves. Scott had to let work now he would need a week off, and I had to let the schools know what was happening and how it might affect the children. I had to fill up the fridge, gas and electric ready for our week away. I had to pack for us three and let Kai's school and school bus know. It was so sudden I had no time to grieve for that baby and I still haven't right up until this day. I shed tears that day and that was it, I had no time and I pushed my feelings to the back of my mind to concentrate on Kai. I had fallen before, this time I would stay strong for us all.

The day came and we made our way to the hospital. We went through the consent forms and had a brief chat, then he had his usual tests ready for later that day. Handing Kai over never gets easier with time, it gets harder. As each time you do it you think this is it, no more, and then you are back where you started. It feels like you are not supposed to be happy, that Kai isn't supposed to have a life with a bit of normality. Every time we handed him over he would always be happy with trusting eyes and my heart would break… if only he knew. We walked around, waiting for the five hours to be over. We went for a drink of diet Coke and a sandwich, but each mouthful just gets lodged in your throat and tastes of guilt. We shouldn't be sitting eating and talking whilst Kai is in there having his head sliced open, it didn't feel right. We walked around the shops, not looking just passing time, we sat in the car, we sat in the hospital,and we went to the shop. Still time ticked by slowly.

Finally the call came. We could go and see our boy, he was in recovery. He was laying there the same as before but this time older and he filled the bed. His soft snoring and his eyes closed under those long fair lashes of his made him look angelic. He looked peaceful. Only the bandages around his head and the tubes snaking in and out of him, the beeps of the machine and the sight of the drain told you different. How many more times were we going to be here? How many more times could we keep putting him through this for a better quality of life? When is enough, enough?

We were home after nearly a week and glad to be back. Beckie had set up FaceTime so we managed to see and speak to the kids most nights when we were in hospital. Kai was happy to sit up and kept trying to lean over the sofa upside down and we had to keep sitting him back. It was about four days after we were home when I left the kids with Scott to go to the shop.

As I walked through the door there was chaos. Scott was shaking holding Kai and there was blood all over the floor and up the wall. The kids were sitting shocked and the dog was licking up the blood. Scott looked up and as he did Kai lifted his head, his whole face was covered in blood and it was coming out of his head fast. "I was sitting right next to Kai and he leant forward off the sofa and before I could grab him he tried to do a roly-poly off the sofa and onto the floor. He's literally just done it!"

I couldn't believe it, Scott held a compress to his head and I phoned for an ambulance. Scott was so upset and blamed himself, but we all know how unpredictable Kai could be and how fast! Scott said he had been sitting with Kai and turned to talk to one of the children when Bailey suddenly said, "Dad, who threw blood at me?" Scott had turned around to see Kai upside down on the floor leaning over the chair.

The ambulance arrived, loaded Kai onto a bed and up the ramp, as soon as the doors were shut Kai burst into hysterical laughter. At that point I was verging on full on panic mode thinking about blood clots and re-stitching, I just looked at him shocked.

"Kai, this is not funny," I scolded, but he was delighted with the response he got from what he had done and just laughed harder wringing his hands together. I could have throttled him at that point from the worry he had just put us through! I was also relieved, though, to see he wasn't in any pain. He laughed all the way to the hospital, lights flashing, whilst poor Scott was sat at home worried sick. The kids were also worried as they had witnessed the whole thing. Luckily, after gluing his head and observing him, Kai was fine and we were allowed home, but he still kept trying to do bloody handstands and roly-polies so we put him in his wheelchair and strapped him in when we left the room. Kai saw this as a challenge and bunny hopped the whole length of the front room with his brakes on, crying with laughter. This boy would be the death of me!

Kai recovered really well those next few weeks and had stopped trying to do gymnastics. He slept a lot more than he had before, but his wounds healed nice and he wasn't in any pain. He was quite content to lay on the sofa with his pillow and quilt and be hand fed food and given sips of water - he was enjoying being the patient this time! He was very quiet those next few weeks and didn't say a word. He would look at us more intently, like his eyes had been opened that bit wider and he was noticing things for the first time. He wanted to be cuddled or hold your hand, and loved snuggling into me whilst the other kids were at school. He enjoyed the peace and quiet.

The kids were good with Kai and were full of questions such as did it hurt? Will he have fits still? Would they need an operation? They kept the noise down a lot and spent a lot of time upstairs or in the garden. I didn't want to lay kai in his room, I wanted him in the family room so he could see us. He was also a little unsteady on his feet so was safer to be in my sight.

I woke up at 4am on a Sunday morning around six weeks after losing the baby and felt the urge to do a pregnancy test. I don't know why, it would be a miracle if I was as obviously bleeding for a week and then in hospital the last thing on our mind had been sex. So in those weeks we had done it once. We had decided that we would have another baby but it would be in the future, once Kai was better. I was waiting for my body to settle and my period to come and would go back on the pill. I went downstairs and pulled out a test, I had one left from when I lost the baby as they came in a pack of two. I peed on the stick, washed my hands and sat waiting in the silent dark. I looked at the stick and two lines appeared one was lightly light, but they were there, a line is a line. I couldn't believe it! Once in six weeks and bam here we were! I ran upstairs, shook Scott awake and told him, we cuddled up together content and fell back into a deep sleep.

My mum was steadily getting worse; she could now no longer chew or swallow food and was basically starving to death. She had no speech left, only the odd word and would have outbursts. She was now in a special hospital type bed at home with my dad, brother and my sister-in-law. She had merely

169

weeks left at the most without food. My dad wanted to get a peg fitted so she would get everything she needed. She could have her fluids food and medication without the risk of chocking. It was a hard choice to make as she was going to eventually die from this cruel disease anyway, but the peg would bring her more time. My dad wasn't ready to let go and he was the one caring for her twenty four hours a day seven days a week. It was his choice, but it was a hard one. I thought it would be kinder to let her go, so we went to see a consultant to see if it was an option before my dad would make the decision. The consultant said they could do it but it was buying time more than anything. This is what my dad wanted to hear. He had been by her side since I was aged two and had stood by her ever since. He washed and dressed her, fed her and took her to hospital appointments with the help of my brother. I can't imagine how it felt for him watching the woman he married and had children with now bedridden. It hurt us all watching her suffer so much over the years, she had lost everything from being able to be a mum and a nan to even being able to use the toilet or chew food. Things we all take for granted.

I visited her with my big bump and she would stare at it and then me as if to say really another one! It was hard on everyone watching the woman we loved go downhill so fast. The peg was fitted and my mum began to gain weight and had some colour in her cheeks, it was still so hard for me to see her like that. In a bed with a nappy and peg, so skinny, just lying there, but I knew time wasn't on her side and I had to push my feeling to the side and see her as she wasn't going to be here forever.

This pregnancy had been the easiest one yet, a few weeks of sickness and nothing like before. I could eat and drink what I wanted and didn't feel tired or achy. It was the best pregnancy and I was happy to stay pregnant! I said to the midwife the pregnancy had been far too easy for me I was sure the birth would be hell! I really wanted a water birth this time, as it was going to be my last baby, I wanted everything calm and had never tried one before. I had my heart set on one.

THE TOUCH OF YOUR HAND

Kai had four seizures over the weeks but they wasn't as aggressive as before, Dr Hank was pleased with his recovery and signed him off from Great Ormond Street care. He would now be seen by our local team, whom I had little faith in. Over the next few weeks Kai had started to sleep a bit more than usual, but after everything he had been through I thought this could be easily explained. He went back to school after a good two months off and would come home shattered.

I got a phone call late one night. My mum had been rushed to hospital with suspected pneumonia, she had aspirated and choked a few times after being sick and gave my dad a few frights. She had gone pale and lifeless one night and he was convinced she was going to die. He had to sit up and watch her as she would choke and have bad episodes. I threw on some clothes and raced straight to the hospital. Her breathing was out of sorts and she was shaking violently, she was moaning in pain. It was hard to watch; my dad was in a real state and my brother, Jamie, was crying, everyone felt so helpless.

She had started to be sick and was bringing up faeces. She was very agitated and scared as she didn't know where she was or what was going on. Every time a nurse came into the room she would scream and shout and lash out. It was heart-breaking as we couldn't even explain to her what was happening as she was in such a state. The doctors didn't really know how to be and were talking about tests they would need to do in front of her, so we had to ask them to tell us outside as she was crying and getting angry.

Seeing my mum like that was when it really hit me for the first time - she was dying, this was it. The disease was in its final stage and I had wasted so many years trying to avoid what was happening by pretending it wasn't. If I didn't see her then it wasn't happening, as much as it hurt I just couldn't handle everything all at once. Yet looking at her lying there in that bed my heart broke, I had wasted precious moments that I could never get back. She looked so vulnerable, almost childlike. She was now around five stone, her leg bones jutted out and her face was frail. She looked like she was dying, I felt protective over her at that moment like the roles had reversed, I was the mum and she was the daughter. I spent most days at the hospital and was there to listen to the consultant; they pulled my dad in a side room and told him that this was it, my mum wasn't going to pull through this. She had developed sepsis too, which was very hard to fight along with pneumonia and how weak she was, it wasn't looking likely she would come through it. I rang the family and they all made their way down to say their goodbyes. Each person went in the room vowing to be strong and each person came out in floods of tears. I hadn't cried yet and was trying to stay strong for my brothers and for my dad.

We had twenty minutes on our own and I held her hand and told her how sorry I was for not always being there and for trying to live in denial. I told her how much I loved her. We sat holding hands in silence and I shed a few tears for us both, for all we had lost and were losing. She had never had the chance to be a nan to my kids not how she wanted to be, we had missed out so much, time had just gone in the blink of an eye.

My mum stayed in hospital for a month, she was too unwell to go home and was on strong medication for pain and drips. But she surprised us all when she was allowed home, my dad didn't want her dying in a hospital, he wanted her at home where she belonged and where she felt safe and loved.

I was due a sweep on my due date. After a few days of on and off contractions it was decided to help bring me along. I was eager to have this baby before Christmas and it was now a week away! I had so much to organise and couldn't bear the thought of being stuck in hospital and the kids waking up to no mummy there! The sweep gave me the odd contraction here and there but nothing to worry about,so the next two days I tried not to think too much of it and just carried on as normal. It was now the 17th December and Scott was getting ready for work, I had contractions but decided not to say anything and let him go.

After putting the kids to bed, I sat down and they got more intense over time and were every ten minutes. I rang Beckie and she rang her mum to be on standby just in case as she was going to be at the birth. Scott came home and by this point they were quite painful, so we rang Dot and made our way to the hospital.

When I got there I'd been having them for around five hours and was tired. I was given an examination and told I was 3cm dilated and hopefully I would have the baby by Christmas. I was shocked - that was a week away, and these contractions were quite regular. She gave me another sweep to move things along. So we made our way back home, deflated. No sooner had I stepped through the threshold, the contractions doubled in intensity. They took my breath away. There was no build up like in previous pregnancies, they were full-on.

Dot took one look at me and said, "I don't care what they say, you are having that baby tonight! I'll stay the night just in case." I decided to have a bath to ease the pain but this did nothing so I got into some fresh pyjamas and climbed into bed. I lay there for about twenty minutes and the contractions were now every five minutes and I was finding it hard to cope with the pain.

"Scott we need to go back now, this baby's coming," I said, shaking him awake. Scott didn't quite believe me as we had just been told hopefully by Christmas, but seeing me trying to walk down the stairs in tears he changed his mind and ran to get the car packed again. I went to the toilet and as I did it filled up with blood. I was in far too much pain to even get any words out at this point so I couldn't tell Scott or Dot and just got straight in the car, concentrating on my breathing.

By the time we got back to the ward I was a sobbing mess, I had never felt pain like this before in all my labours, the contractions were excruciating. The midwife's took one look at me and got me straight in the pool and Scott rang Beckie to tell her to get here fast. I was gulping down the gas and air and looked up to see Beckie was standing there! All of a sudden I heard a midwife say, "I can see the head!" I was over the moon this was going much faster than I thought! I could barely concentrate I was so high but I then heard, "It's not the head, it's blood." Apparently the pool filled with blood. I was dragged out of the pool, put in a wheelchair and rushed down to the consultant lead unit all whilst protesting I needed the pool. I was screaming in pain at this point and was given an epidural, but it didn't work, I could feel every single pain and it didn't feel natural. I honestly lost control at this point and couldn't come back from it. I was in a state of panic convinced I was going to die as the pain was too much.

Finally, I was pushing and I can honestly say it was the worst pain of my life, I couldn't understand why it felt so different than before. Then the midwife said, "The baby is back to back." It all made sense; I had heard they were one of the worst labours. As I was pushing, Scott later said, it was like something

176

from the exorcist as the baby was spinning trying to get into position. Finally after one last push baby Lola Violet Hammond came into the world weighing 7lb 12ozs. Like Daisy, she was Scott's double, same nose, eyes and bottom lip. I was smitten instantly. Here was the baby that wasn't supposed to be, that was never planned for.

The birth had left me with a lump which was explained as a hematoma from the traumatic labour, I was told it would shrink in time. But over the days it grew and was now the size of half a melon I couldn't sit down, lay down or move as I was in agony. When my baby cried Scott had to deal with her, I felt utterly useless. Day four I woke up freezing cold but was burning up, my teeth were chattering and I was in immense pain, so Scott took me to the hospital. I was told I would need an operation, but it was the day before Christmas Eve, there was no way I was staying in hospital! So I refused and was given antibiotics to deal with the infection I now had. Scott did everything that day from cooking to bathing the children and the housework. I woke up the next day and felt no pain; it had burst in the night! I was so happy it was Christmas Eve and I could now prepare for the next day without being in constant pain.

I tried to visit my mum as much as I could, I knew time was short so when the children went back to school I took Lola to see her. She was lying in bed connected to drips and hoists above her a special chair in the corner. My dad rarely left her side and was sleeping in the front room, her breathing would become shallow at times and he would think this was it and then she would breathe again.

I lifted Lola up onto the bed in her car seat and put her right next to her Nanny. "This is Lola, Mum," I said. My mum was awake and stared at my belly and then at the baby and she smiled, she was pulling at the car seat to get her out so she could see her properly and grabbing to touch her. Then she said, "Lo-la" I couldn't believe it!

"Dad, did you hear that? She said Lola!" We stood smiling, tears in our eyes grateful for the fact that she had got to live to see this moment. The next time I went to see her with Lola she just stared ahead, I looked at my dad. "She doesn't seem herself." He said he thought it was the drugs, as she was now on morphine which the nurses would come in everyday to administer. I looked at her and she didn't acknowledge me or Lola, the light had gone from her eyes there was nothing there. I knew it wouldn't be long before the angels came for her.

Kai started to sleep more than usual and at the beginning of February I was really concerned that this wasn't normal, so I took him to the doctors who said he had an infection. He was given some antibiotics but he just couldn't shake it off. By the middle of February I was still worried he hadn't improved, he had been sleeping more since January, but now it was all day. He would have to be carried out of bed and he would sleep whilst we showered him and dressed him. Where he used to stay up all day, I would now have to wake him for lunch and he would eat and then go back to sleep until dinner time, then eat, then go to bed. This wasn't normal and I took him back to the doctors who ran some blood tests, they came back as borderline thyroid problem and vitamin D deficiency and were given some vitamin medicine to perk him up. I thought this would take some time to get into his system, so we waited to see if this had an effect. The doctor also wanted him back in three weeks for another blood test.

My dad phoned me and said the words I had heard the few months before, it was time to say goodbye. Mum had gone downhill very quickly, her breathing wasn't good and she was sleeping a lot more. He had been told she had a week at the most; I went over when the kids were at school. I didn't want them to see her or have the image of her as their last memory. I walked in and it was like seeing a completely different person in front of me. She was just so thin I could see her bones poking out, her skin was very pale and she was fast asleep. Her breathing was very shallow. Her hair was bald at the back where she had been lying in the bed so long, like when a baby when they shed their hair at the back. She had bed sores and she looked like there was no more life left in her, she had no fight left and nothing left to give.

The atmosphere was tense, my dad and brother were red eyed from crying, and I thought I could stay strong for them. I walked over, took her hand and just watched her for a few minutes. I had to leave the room I couldn't breathe in there everything was closing in around me and I went into the kitchen. My dad followed and we both broke down holding onto each other, we didn't speak there was nothing to say. I stayed in there for a good ten minutes and composed myself enough to go back into the room. I sat back down and just looked everywhere but at her, if I didn't look it wasn't happening. But my protection technique was failing me, she was in front of me and this was it, she was dying. I kissed her one last time, I stroked her hair and held her hand. "Bye, Mum, I love you."

In my head I was willing her to let go, to see someone you love have to endure years of losing the ability to do all the things we take for granted. Walk, sit, talk, lift your head, go to the toilet, or eat. This illness had deprived her of everything and I despised it, I hated it with a passion and I was very angry. Like my mum said in that room all those years ago when we got told the news Kai could have TS - why? Why us?

The days went by and I would ring for updates, I couldn't go back I didn't want to see her take her last breath; I didn't want to be there. I had said my goodbyes and now all I could do was wait. As each day passed I wondered if perhaps she would prove them all wrong again, perhaps she would pull through. I was just walking out of the door to collect the kids from school when Scott called me back. "Vikki, phone."

"Who is it?" I was in a rush, I had no time to talk to anyone I would be late for collecting the kids.

"It's your brother, Jamie," he said and he couldn't look at me.

I walked back up the driveway, I knew this was it. "Hello?" I said.

There was silence for a few seconds and then he said,"She's gone." I didn't know what emotion to feel first - relief that she wasn't suffering anymore, sad that she died so young, or angry that she missed so much. I was silent. "She just stopped breathing a few minutes ago," he continued.

I told him I loved him, there was nothing more we could say to each other.

The next few days were weird, I busied myself with trying to get to the bottom of what was wrong with Kai. Scott booked a few days off work as he didn't want to leave me, I cried the day she died as I was shocked, I couldn't believe she was gone. I knew she was dying, I had years to get used to the idea, but now she wasn't here anymore I was shocked. Scott was helping me with everything, as was Beckie, they were expecting me to break down, but I couldn't. Scott kept saying 'you can cry, it's OK to cry, please just cry on me', but no tears would come. I just felt angry, angry at the world, and I was going to use that anger to get to the bottom of what was wrong with Kai.

Kai was now at his worst, he was asleep all day and night by now and even the school was concerned. He had a constant cold and was full of snot and had a terrible cough. He was diagnosed with a chest infection and given antibiotics,which again did nothing for him. So he had another blood test, this time they showed his platelets were lower than last time and another blood test was arranged for the next two weeks' time.

The school were very concerned, as was I, but it felt like I wasn't being listened to. My doctor was great and did all he could his end and referred us to a haematologist. We had an appointment for a paediatrician who asked lots of questions and, again, said we needed to see a haematologist, we explained

181

we were waiting for the referral. Kai was really bad by now and couldn't walk or chew his food or even lift his head. I was basically looking after a coma patient; he had no life in him at all and could barely sit up. I felt like I was banging my head against a brick wall, every time I rang to chase up the referral I was told I would be called back, or put through to the wrong department, or was left leaving messages on answer machines. His blood tests came back and his platelets had dropped yet again. Kai was as white as a sheet, he lost all of his speech and signing, and was off school a lot as he just slept the day away. I was at my wits end with no one caring! I felt like they just thought oh well he's disabled anyway so what's the rush? I was certain if it was any of my other children they would have been seen straight away.

My mum's funeral is a bit of a blur to me. We went over to my dad's house to wait for the funeral cars to take us to the crematorium. My dad had my mum in an open coffin and everyone was going in to pay their respects. I didn't want to go in but felt like I had to, I made Scott go in first to tell me how she looked, as I didn't want to see her looking frightened if that makes sense. He came back out with tears in his eyes and said, "She looks peaceful, Vikki, but it's up to you."

My dad said he would ask everyone to leave the room as he knows what I'm like showing emotion, especially in public. After ringing Beckie and talking to her I decided to go in and say goodbye. I stood in the hallway whilst everyone left the room; I was shaking with fear and also trying to hold my emotions in. I walked in the room and she was lying in a coffin, she looked so frail and childlike. She had her jock teddy with her and a hat to cover her thinning hair. She was so pale but all the worry and frown lines had gone, making her look so much younger than her forty-eight years. I stood in the corner; I didn't want to touch her, I didn't want to feel her cold. The last time I held her hand she was warm and I didn't want this as a last memory. I stood and a huge sense of sadness washed over me, she was so young and this disease had robbed her of so many years. Just then I felt some arms around me and I turned around and cuddled my dad and Scott. I just couldn't believe this was it, she was actually gone.

Seeing so many people at the crematorium was a huge comfort to me, my dad was overwhelmed but was holding it in. My brothers, Thomas and Jamie were also holding on to their emotions. I walked in and instantly heard her song 'Orinoco Flow' by Enya just as her coffin was revealed by the opening curtains. Her coffin was so small and hearing that song that I used to shout at her to turn off playing took me back to her standing in the kitchen singing at the top of her voice. I cried, but wiped the tears away before we were seated. Before I knew it I was called up to do my reading, I was determined to tell people how she was before she became ill. I got to line three and seeing all the people in front of me, my young brothers, who were robbed of their mum at such a young age, my dad who was robbed of his wife, I broke. Tears stung my eyes as I struggled and fought to keep them in, not now, not in front of everyone, but a ball rose to my throat and I couldn't talk, no words would come out. I tried to compose myself but

I just couldn't speak as tears fell onto the page, I was angry with myself. I wanted to do this one thing for my mum, just then I felt hands around my waist and I looked up and saw Scott by my side. "You can do this," he whispered. That was all I needed, and I swallowed down the ball of grief wiped my eyes and continued with my words.

I wanted to say a few words about my mum, the mum Thomas and Jamie and I knew before she became ill. Mum was a feisty character, not one for hugs or kisses but if anyone dared mess with her family, boy did they know it. She had fighting spirit right up until the end. The way I like to remember her is dancing around the kitchen to Ska music or UB40 or Enya. She kept us all in line (even my dad) with the 'look', or gave chase. Funny memories I have are of her throwing shepherd's pie- complete with the plate - at my dad, and then getting the hump because she realised it was her dinner she threw! Hitting the next door neighbour, and making us watch the same Brad Pitt films over and over again. The time when I really saw her soft side was when she was beside me as I gave birth to her first grandchild, Kai. She was there for everything and worshipped the ground he walked on. The thing I am most sad about is how she was robbed of so much, so young. She missed out on so much, even though she was here she wasn't the Pauline we all knew her. Although she would still flip the finger at the poor nurses! One thing I can say about my mum is she had strength; she was strong and defied the doctors so many times. She may have been small but she fought right up until her last breath with her hubby at her side, and her blue eyed boy, Jamie (as we used to wind her up and say). She cherished her husband, our dad, and he looked after her right through every stage of her illness. She is with her own mum now, at peace, and there is no need to keep fighting, she can rest. For a small person she has left a very large hole in our hearts. Sleep well, Mum x

WHAT ARENT YOU TELLING ME?

I was at my wits end and rang the out of hours' doctors, after getting a call back I was told to buy some nasal spray for Kai. I hung up. By the Monday morning I'd had enough and rang to find out what was going on with my appointment for Kai. The consultant haematologist had left, hence no appointment, which meant more waiting. I was livid! By now Kai was coming up in really angry bruises from his feet to his chest, I was terrified. I instantly thought he had leukaemia. I was also scared as I thought someone would think that I was hurting him and was going to take him away from me. I got myself in a real state every time a new bruise appeared and made sure I let the school and doctor know as I was so paranoid. Kai went back for more blood tests which, again, came back as low platelets, even lower than the last time! No one could say why, just wanted to repeat the blood tests. I felt like screaming, I went home and went straight on google typing in all of Kai's symptoms. If no one would help me I would find out what was wrong myself! As I typed them in Leukaemia flashed up, I rang the blood nurse in a real state. I was convinced he had cancer and they were hiding it from me, she assured me that he didn't have cancer at all but they didn't know what was going on.

One morning at breakfast Kai was sitting up with my support as I fed him some toast, I had cut it up small for him to get into his mouth and swallow, as he was now having trouble with chewing. As I gave him his last piece I walked him into the front room and he began to cough, I realised he was choking. So tried to remove the bit in his mouth but it wouldn't budge, I whacked his back but still it wouldn't budge and I screamed for Scott. Just as I did Kai started to go blue and collapsed on the floor, Scott put his hand in his mouth and pulled the whole bit of toast out. I was terrified and shaking but Kai seemed unaffected and crawled back to the sofa to sleep.

I had no time to grieve for my mum and still haven't to this day, every day we were faced with a new problem, I now had to lift Kai everywhere and he is a big twelve-year-old, very solid. It was killing my back. I had to sit with him to feed him and wake him to give him drinks. I had to stop bathing him and only shower him as he would fall asleep in the bath. I was given a meeting at the school with a whole team of people about Kai and how he had been lately. As we sat in the room and talked I could see they were just as concerned as me. They wanted to use hoists on

Kai at school now as they couldn't carry him, which was understandable. They wanted to use a walking frame to stand him up straight, as he was bent double lately. They also wanted me to have an occupational therapist (OT) out to our home to see what equipment Kai needed. They felt he needed hoists and tracking fitted so I wouldn't have to lift him anymore. Tears threatened to escape my eyes but I held them back, I refused the hoists. Kai was going to get better; he didn't need all this. Having all of this equipment was like I was accepting that he would be this way forever, and I wasn't willing to. I could see the pity in their eyes as I refused any help but agreed the OT could come to my home. I could see they thought I was in denial. I knew my boy would get better I just had to find out what was causing all of this!

A week after the toast incident, Kai was worse than ever, it was a Sunday afternoon and as I tried to wake him up to feed him he wouldn't even open his eyes. I rang the out of hours' doctor who came out to check on him. He took his temperature which was slightly high but not enough to cause alarm. His stats were low and he said he wanted him in hospital to be checked over today as he thought he might have an infection.

"OK, I will pack his stuff and get over there," I said.

"No," the doctor said, "I'm calling an ambulance." In a strange way I was happy, surely being in hospital someone would now take me seriously and discover what was causing all of this to happen to my boy?

At the hospital he was checked over and his temperature had gone down, I explained everything over the months that had happened. The bruising, the lack of any skills, the sleeping, and the choking. He was given an x-ray and we were told to wait. By two o'clock in the morning we were still sat waiting and nothing was being done, I got angry and told them I was taking him home. I was livid he had been there nine hours and just sat waiting. Monday morning came and I took the kids to school but kept Kai off, I was going to take him to my doctors as I wasn't happy with the way he was. As I got back from the school run the local hospital rang and said they needed us to come straight in, they had just got the x-ray results back and Kai had something in his lung. He also had pneumonia.

We rushed straight back to the hospital, we were shown the x-rays which was showing that Kai had aspirated on something, which would have been the toast. He had pneumonia but we had caught it in time for it not to have been serious. He was given some very strong antibiotics, and we were allowed to go home. They didn't know why his platelets were low, and when we got the blood test results back from the previous day they had dropped to 88. Considering platelets should be between 150 and 400, I was terrified. Yet no one had any answers. We went home and I sat on Google, I found a condition which caused platelets to drop and it was caused by medication. I also went online to chat to some special needs mums who had been through similar experiences. A lady got back to me who said her son had had leukocytopnia, which was caused by the medication he was on and

189

had started to slowly poison his body and his platelets had dropped so low he needed blood transfusions. I had found the answer, I knew this was what Kai had, I now just had to prove it.

I voiced my concerns about what I knew was making Kai so ill, it was his medication sodium valporate, the doctor couldn't touch his medication, it had to be done by a consultant. My consultant was insistent it was infection and to give him a few weeks to get over his pneumonia. She arranged for an MRI to rule out any more growths in his tumours and another blood test for two weeks' time. I was terrified Kai wouldn't make it; I knew he was so unwell his body wouldn't keep going, he didn't have time but no one would listen. I told Beckie and Scott and the school that I was scared I would lose Kai; all my old fears came back to the surface. If Kai wasn't here, then I couldn't be either, I couldn't live with the pain of him not in my life. I knew something was wrong but everyone around me said it wouldn't come to that, he wouldn't die. I thought perhaps it was me? Should I give him time? Was I overreacting?

We went to Kai's MRI appointment but before he could have it we were asked if he had any metal clips in his head. "Of course not, we would have been told," I said, even so they wanted to look through his notes and last scan to check. They couldn't find them so they asked if we would take Kai for an x-ray before having the MRI, just to be safe, so off we went. Once he had the x-ray we went back to wait for the MRI, then we were asked to have a repeated x-ray as they could see something on the pictures. My heart sank, Scott and I looked at each other terrified as we were led back into the room. After the x-ray I asked to look at the results. They showed me on the screen it was showing up a handful of little paperclip type images. We were certain he hadn't had clips and were left terrified they had been left in his brain after surgery by mistake. The doctors couldn't get hold of the hospital to check and so we were sent home to wait as they couldn't do the MRI in case it was metal, in which case it would be very dangerous to do an MRI as the machine acts like a magnet and would pull whatever was in Kai's head, I felt useless on the way home. Did they say he had clips and we overlooked it? I looked back through his notes and could find no record and I knew I hadn't been told. I was so worried those next days as I rung around hospitals trying to find out what was in my son's head. Scott was climbing the walls with the waiting. I finally got hold of someone from Great Ormond Street and was told that the surgeon was in the middle of retiring and they couldn't see anything in Kai's notes to suggest he should have clips in his head. So we had to wait until Friday to find out, as they were going to be having a meeting to get to the bottom of it all.

Friday came and I rang back first thing, I was relieved to hear the clips were titanium and were safe for an MRI, they were also supposed to be in his head, but had not been put in the notes. I was over the moon. I had been imagining more surgery and all sorts of scenarios! An MRI was booked for the following week and in the meantime he had more blood tests done. Kai was now off school, he couldn't go as he was just lifeless so there was no point in sending him. His nose would run all day long even though he had recovered from his pneumonia.

The school were amazing and were fighting with me to get appointments to have him see a haematologist, and both of us were feeling like Kai had just been left to get on with it. Kai's blood test results came back and were showing his platelets were now 71, with no signs of going up. His clotting came back as low and there was a huge concern that if he were to have a seizure and bang himself he would bleed and it wouldn't stop. The school refused to have him as they were scared, and yet so was I. Every day I had to watch him like a hawk, I was so frightened of him falling, I would feed him in the front room, all the food was cut into tiny pieces and I hand fed him. He still could barely swallow and with every mouthful my heart would thump away waiting for him to choke.

I could no longer bathe him as he would fall asleep in the bath and I struggled to get him out of the bath on my own. I was terrified to shower him on my own as he could no longer support himself in anyway and I was unable to keep him upright and wash him safely. It took two of us to shower him; it was breaking my heart to see him like this. Why was nobody listening to me? It felt like when he was a baby and I was basically told I was imagining it all. After a while you start to believe them, you become so beaten down and worn out. I was finding it hard to eat, sleep or function and would obsess over Kai. We could no longer take him out as he was so cold and just slept slumped over. When he was awake it was only to have a seizure or eat a few mouthfuls of food.

The occupational therapist came out, Beckie and Scott stayed with me as I was emotionally beaten down at this point. I had it in my head they would think I couldn't cope with him or I was harming him in some way. We sat in my front room, Kai fast asleep in the corner full of snot and coughing. They were shocked to see the decline in him, and asked how I was coping. I became defensive and said I was coping fine, even though I just wanted to break down and say actually not at all, I was terrified to be left alone with Kai. If he fell, or choked or had a long seizure I just wouldn't be able to cope with it. But I couldn't say any of those things through pure fear of Kai being taken. Then came the talk, I knew what they were here for, equipment. They wanted to put tracking and hoists and slings and shower and bath chairs. They wanted the tracking to run from Kai's room to the bathroom. I refused, no way. Kai was not going to decline like my mum did, he was going to get better I told them. I felt everyone's eyes on me and pity too. They thought I was in denial about Kai and told me I would need it eventually as he was getting bigger and stronger and carrying him like I was doing was no good for my safety. I didn't care what they thought Kai was going to get better I was going to get my boy back. Enough of the beaten down, worn out mess I had become, I was going to fight this.

Kai's MRI scan came back as normal, and I was more convinced than ever that it was the medication. I rang the school in a complete rage and spoke to the nurse. I told her to tell the consultant not to send me anymore appointments she wasn't listening to me at all, I'd had enough I was at breaking point. I was going to sell anything I could to take Kai to a private hospital, the nurse completely understood and said she would pass the message on. I rang our local private hospital and explained what was happening, I was being ignored and Kai had been unwell for eight months now and still no haematologist appointment. She explained it would be a few sessions with a paediatrician and bloods, the total would come to nearly £1,000, and they had no haematologist.

This option would not suit us as we needed a blood doctor to look at his bloods to see why he had gone downhill so quickly. I was told if Kai bled he would need blood transfusions, as it wouldn't clot and yet here we were with no support and no one to hear us. I was at bursting point now, ready to fight, I rang the school back and told them I was taking Kai off his medication myself, I'd had enough of waiting to see what happened and would they pass this onto the consultant for me. If anything were to happen to Kai whilst he was being weaned off his medication with no support from consultants I wanted them to know it was their fault.

The nurse was great and straight away got onto the local consultant who rang me straight back. Funny that. "Mrs Hammond, can I ask why you are looking into private health care for Kai?" the consultant asked.

All the anger from the last few months boiled over."Because you are failing him! You are not listening to me! I KNOW it's the medication that is causing this. Yet you keep telling me it's an infection.

I have had no hospital appointments just repeated blood tests with no one to look at them and tell me what the hell is wrong!" I shouted.

There was a pause and then she said, "We think it is infection and not the medication as that is a very rare side effect. Are you planning on taking Kai off the medication as I would strongly advise against this."

"I'm not planning on taking him off the medication, I AM taking him off it and I'm starting today. If I am wrong, no harm will be done he can go back onto it but I am not waiting to see what happens next. I am not waiting to see my boy in hospital having blood transfusions, I am trying this now. Also, have you referred me back to Dr James like I have been asking for months?" I snapped.

"I will phone him now and ring you straight back," she said and hung up. I sat shaking with rage, *I don't care what anyone says,* I thought, *enough is enough, no more waiting.* The phone rang ten minutes later and I snatched it up.

"Mrs Hammond, I have spoken to Dr James I have referred you back to him. He says to get Kai off that medication now." I felt so relieved. *At last* someone was listening to me and I knew he would, I knew the referral for him hadn't been put through, but I would deal with that later. I listened as she gave me weaning off medication plan and was grinning from ear to ear as I rang Scott and Beckie to tell them the news.

Straight away I dropped the dosage; it would have to be done over six weeks until he was completely off it. If it was the medication we should

195

start to see results pretty much soon after. The next few days Kai could lift his head up. The next few weeks, Kai was able to sit, to stand and to walk. He began to eat more than he ever had and could chew again. It was like watching a miracle happen, like he was coming back to me. By the end of the six weeks he was completely off the medication and completely back to normal. He went back to school, his nose stopped running, his voice came back and he was more alert than ever before. He would shout so loudly "Mum, Dad, Beck!" He started signing 'thank you' and 'more' again, and he had a new sentence, his first and probably his only sentence he would ever say, "My bubba, Lola."

He became obsessed with Lola like he was seeing her for the first time, he had ignored all of the other children, but he had a huge bond with Lola. If she cried he would sit with her and stare into her eyes and say Bubba. He would pat her head and kiss her, if I put her to bed he would walk around the house looking for her shouting "Bubba Lola!" every single day I woke up I felt like I had won the lottery, I was walking around with a big stupid grin on my face. People must have thought I was mad, I had just lost my mum and here I was happy as anything. I was happy my boy was back and better than ever. He would not need hoists or tracking or bath or shower aides, he did not need slings or walking frames. He was walking and jumping on the trampoline and everyday he came home from school he would go straight outside and sit on his little swing chair smiling, and I would smile with him with tears in my eyes. He had won another battle.

I had no time to grieve those next few months and still haven't to this day, I think I did my grieving when my mum was declining so quickly, now I just feel an overwhelming sense of sadness and emptiness. But one look at Kai on his swing chair it turns into a smile, I have so much to be blessed about.

EVERY BREATH YOU TAKE

Family life with a child with disabilities can be very
challenging, it is very hard to get the right balance
and although we try our best it must be hard on the
other children. They never complain that we can't
just get into the car and go out, they never moan that
routine has to be rigid, they just accept it. Although
every day they ask questions such as, will Kai ever
move out or be a father? Will he ever drive or be able
to talk? I answer them as honestly as I can–no, Kai
will never live independently, he will always need
Mummy and Daddy to care of him, to dress and
change his nappy, to wash him to feed him. To make
sure he is safe and to care for him when he has a
seizure. I can see this hurts them, they understand he
will never have the opportunities they have. He will
never ride a bike, or read a book, he will never have a
conversation or watch a film, but they also
understand that through him we have learnt so much,

we have learnt how to be patient. We have learnt that everyone is different and we should be thankful we have full use of our healthy bodies. They have learned how to be tolerant when all they want to do is watch TV in peace! They go to groups and have friends around as much as they can so they get their time. This wouldn't be possible, though, without the help of Beckie. She will watch Kai whilst I drop Bailey off to his clubs and Honey-Mae to hers, whilst I take Daisy to parties. Kai doesn't like change very much, he knows when he gets in from school he has his dinner and his bath and a little nap on the sofa, Scott goes to work and I am housebound. If it wasn't for the hours Beckie puts in, my children would probably not have the social life's they do.

It is hard for me to balance everything, to be a mum to five children with five sets of different needs, to be a cook, a cleaner, a chauffeur and a wife. Sometimes your marriage is pushed to the side – Scott and I rarely go out. It is hard to get childcare especially for someone as complex as Kai. Also I have trust issues so I wouldn't leave him with just anyone. Although Scott and I have no social life's at all, Friday nights are our nights, we usually put the kids to bed and once he's home from work we have a takeaway and snuggle up to a DVD. Saturday nights are family nights with the kids.

I can see why marriages become strained and a high percentage of married couples with a special need child split up. It *is* hard. The worrying, the stress, the arguing, the not knowing and the lack of time for each other. The choices you have to make, sometimes in complete disagreement with each other, the hospital stays and then of course the financial strain it all brings.

Support is another factor that rings a huge strain on you, the lack of consultants listening to you, the constant fighting for tests, results and equipment. Even nappies are a cause to fight - we are only issued with three nappies a day. Of course, Kai is twelve now so doesn't fit in the normal sized nappies and buying them are four times the price of a normal pack of nappies. The false promises from social workers, that never lead to anything. The unwanted advice from professionals that, in reality, have no clue what we're going through. The lack of local facilities for a child like Kai, the ignorance of people that have no clue what it is like to have a disabled child. Some families have little or no support at all. We, for instance, have never had a family support worker or an epilepsy nurse. We have no faith in our local hospital or team. We have to travel to see a doctor from the hospital we trust. Fighting to get a doctor to do a home visit when it is near enough impossible for you to get your child to the doctors. The list is endless, but I am very lucky I have a great husband and great friends like Beckie, Ria, Sarah, Corina and Amy. Those you can turn to on your very dark days, when you feel like the world is against you, and then there is my online family, who are amazing with their advice and hold a very special place in my heart.

The biggest fear of us mums is not being listened to and heard, but also the risk of shouting too loud and bringing attention to ourselves. A huge fear in many mums of a special need child is if they admit they are struggling then the child will be taken away.

As dramatic as this sounds, it is how we feel, to admit to struggling with your child's everyday care and needs we fear that it is looked on as 'not coping'.

I think people I know seeing Kai for the first time shocks them, I can see the look of pity in their face and the relief that it isn't them that has a child with a disability. Some friends of mine confide in me with their problems and then automatically apologise with, "Sorry, I know it's not as bad as what you are going through." But everyone has problems, I don't see Kai as a problem and I know they don't mean that, they mean the situation. Everyone has their own problems and no ones are worse than anyone else's. My friends are great with Kai and treat him like any other child, Beckie will tell him off just like she does her own and that's the way it should be. I like that Kai is treated the same, as I know he knows a lot more than he lets on!

It is hard for some people to understand, especially family members, if we have been invited to certain events it is hard for us. As much as we love the invite and the thought, it isn't always possible to go. For one, night time is a problem as we have no one to watch the children and they have to be confident with Kai too; two, if the kids are invited and we take Kai, we have to think about where it is, is there access for the wheelchair? Is it loud and busy? (Kai hates loud music and busy places.) What food will be served? (As Kai will only eat certain coloured dry food.) When we do manage to go we have to work around Kai's routine. If we are invited to someone's home this is a big problem, are there stairs there? Things on the sides? Breakables? Kai is like a

201

mini tornado and can smash up a place pretty quickly, so we have to turn down a lot of invitations. Obviously, we try our best to work around it but it is very difficult and I don't think many people understand how stressful it can be.

The six week holidays we try to do as much as we can with the kids, especially when Kai is due for surgery. That year we took them to LEGOLAND, Gulliver's land and Chessington World of Adventure. Kai loves the thrill of fast rides and I usually get dragged on with him and Bailey. Day trips can be very stressful with other people's ignorant attitudes. When we go we get given a pass where we can wait at an exit of any ride to avoid the queues. This is because Kai can't stand up for very long and needs to be in his wheelchair right up until we are going on the ride. He doesn't like waiting for long and can become angry, and also it is unsafe due to his seizures to stand for a long period in case he drops to the floor. Also his autism makes it harder for him to understand about waiting and this can cause tantrums. We have had dirty looks when we wait at the exit with our pass and people whisper or comment.

One time we walked on through the exit and Scott was carrying Kai up the slope to go onto the ride. A woman who was next in line and had obviously been waiting for a long time became very angry and said loudly behind me, "That's right you push in, there is a queue here you know!"

I looked at her and stopped walking. "Is there? Oh, I just thought I'd push right in!" I said to her in a sarcastic tone.

"Well try waiting like we have been all of this time," she spat.

Just then Scott stopped walking and put Kai down. "Our son is disabled, you arsehole, do you not think we would love nothing more than to queue alongside you? You stupid woman."

She looked at her husband for support and he put his head down and whispered to her to shut up. "Well you could still queue," she said.

How we kept our cool I will never know, she was completely ignorant and unaware of how hard it can be with a wheelchair in a queue that has narrow entrances and stairs. We don't let people like that spoil our day. Scott gave her a real mouthful and I just looked at her and shook my head. People's attitudes actually disgust me sometimes.

I think the press fuel a lot of these negative thoughts against the disabled. So many people have been caught claiming what they are not entitled to and been caught out faking an illness to gain the 'benefit's' of being disabled. Of course if you are not disabled a blue badge, a car, monetary benefits, and a queue pass is an attractive package. But if you actually *are* disabled these are things to make your life that little bit easier when everyday life is such a struggle. People need to remember that next time they see a child in a wheelchair going on a ride before they do.

I went to see Donna for peace of mind, she told me that she could see Kai being offered a drug of some sort from abroad and he would be on it by November time. She said he would do really well on this drug and to go ahead with it. She said she could feel my mum's spirit around Kai, protecting him; she knew things I had said to myself and personal thoughts I had told nobody. I loved seeing Donna she instantly makes me feel better about everything,

Kai was now back to normal and doing really well, he is now signing and saying the odd word and generally loves life. He's always smiling and can be found in the garden on his swing chair or asleep in weird positions throughout the house. He loves swimming and food, the trampoline and school. His seizures made a reappearance not long after we got him off that medication, he started having around six a day, which is not bad considering he was having thirty-plus a day. We got an appointment with the consultant, we love to discuss our options. We obviously couldn't go down the VNS or ketogenic diet path. Surgery is not an option he's had far too much for my liking in his short life. Medication could be added or adjusted which I was less trusting of… and then he mentioned a drug trial.

He was offering the chance of Kai going on the everolimus trial, they were recruiting children with TS.

Everolimus is a drug that can reduce the number of epileptic seizures in people who have epilepsy associated with Tuberous Sclerosis Complex. It works by blocking a protein that acts as an important regulator of tumour cell growth. Findings from previous studies have shown that there were fewer seizures in patients with active epilepsy and have shown to shrink growths due to TSC, it can also help with autism. 345 patients with TSC will join the study from around the world. We were told that if we accepted we would have to keep a six week seizure diary for Kai. We would also go in eleven times for two hours a time over a six month period.

Once we had listened we did some research of our own and also spoke to other families whose children were on the study or had been. Every story I heard filled me with more hope, we had to try this for Kai. His seizures are now very strong and he drops to the floor or against walls and smashes his head. They are starting to last longer and increasing every week, so we have little choice but to try this; it is literally our last hope.

We went along to the appointment and Kai had to have his bloods taken and his weight and height. We had to take a urine sample, which involved me syringing wee from his nappy at five o clock in the morning which was fun! Kai, who normally refuses to cooperate with any sort of test at all, was an absolute angel that day! He let them take bloods, he let them weigh him and even stood straight to be measured. He had an ECG done and sat still for his blood pressure. It got me wondering - did Kai realise we were trying to help him? It seemed weird how well behaved he was that day! I then had to answer a whole booklet of questions and then do a phone questionnaire.

Once they had all looked at the results whilst I fed Kai toast, crisps and chocolate – he was starving from having to have nothing to eat for his blood tests! They called us both into the room and announced that Kai *was* eligible for the trial and would start 17th November 2014! I was thrilled and so was Scott. We have heard such amazing results that we are hoping it helps Kai too.

As I write this we are keeping a seizure diary and every day they seem to be going up, so we know we have made the right decision. Kai will go back in November and will either be given the actual drug or a placebo, we won't know which he has and neither will the doctors. We will all find out next year together. Every week he will have to be in Cambridge at 8.30 to be monitored and assessed to make sure he isn't reacting in any way. The main side effect can be mouth ulcers and I am praying this doesn't happen. Kai needs a break, he needs a good year off hospitals and seizures.

I sometimes look back and wish I had made the most of those seizure free years after his surgery. But the thing with TSC is, it gives you false hope, just as you get used to a normal life something crops up! Once we find out which drug Kai was given he will get the everolimus drug regardless for around two years, after that, who knows? It is a constant round of waiting, hoping and praying that we have made the right choice. Kai is also due a kidney scan any time now, and again we just have to hope his lumps haven't grown.

Although this book has been very dark in places, and I have agonised over if I should have been so honest in places, I felt Kai's story needed to be told. I wanted everyone who has ever been too afraid to ask me the questions they wanted to know to understand what it is like to be Kai's mum. I want to educate those who have ever judged a person with disabilities to see just how much of a battle every day

206

for them is already, without ignorance. Although I am not speaking for every special need's mum out there, everyone's story and experiences are completely different. I am simply speaking as a mum to a very special little boy. A little boy that has taken me on a very special journey over the years, and every single experience has taught me so much.

I know that life is short; we don't know what is around the corner, and to make every day count. I know that the constant battles and fighting are exhausting, but we keep on as we are our child's voice. I know that every sly or ignorant comment cuts deep, but we carry on head held high because our child does. I know there are a lot of other families out there that are going through similar or worse times than you and are only too happy to listen to you. I know that the bond you have with your children is so strong you will get through everything thrown at you to make their life easier. I know that when you feel like you cannot take anymore you will find strength from somewhere - use that strength to fight! I know that when you feel that something is wrong and everyone else is telling you different, to listen to your gut and your heart. Never ever take someone else's word for it; if we had done that, Kai wouldn't be here today. I know that without Kai my life wouldn't be as it is today, I wouldn't be the person I am today if it wasn't for him. He has taught me so much, he is my hero and when I am having a bad day I look at him and try to pull myself together. If he can come through all he has without a single complaint then I have no right to sit and wallow.

I agonised over revealing my dark days in this book but felt I needed to, I need people to understand how it was at our worst times so they can understand why every day is now a blessing.

I chose the title 'Whenever I Fall' as I personally fell in places and needed to find my feet again. Through the dark times, to the battles, and then to the good times. It is also a line from the Ronan Keating song When You Say Nothing At All. This song was playing when we had Kai's scan and found out there was a problem, it was also our wedding song. Scott has even got the lyrics tattooed up him arm. It is a very special song to us and hearing it, depending on what mood I am in, can bring back certain emotions.

I know I can never make plans as Kai will be with me for life. And although he will grow in size and hopefully improve a little over time he will rely on me for everything. He is my little Peter Pan living in Never Land - he will grow old, but mentally he will stay a child forever. He will never feel loss or pain or stress at work or worry about money, and when I look at it like that I smile to myself. That does not sound like a bad life to me.

Although I am certain we will have many more battles to face over the next few years, I know I am now strong enough to cope with them. As long as I have my family by my side and my boy leading us, I know we will be fine. I don't know what the future holds and I don't want to know, looking far ahead scares me and so we simply take one day at a time.

THE END

Printed in Great Britain
by Amazon